From the Kwai
to the Kingdom

From the Kwai to the Kingdom

Andy Milliken

with a foreword by
Canon Michael Harper

Marshalls

Marshalls Paperbacks
Marshall Pickering
3 Beggarwood Lane, Basingstoke, Hants, RG23 7LP, UK
A subsidiary of the Zondervan Corporation

First published by Marshall Morgan & Scott Ltd.

British Library Cataloguing in Publication Data

Milliken, Andy
  From the Kwai to the Kingdom.
  1. World War, 1939–1945——Prisoners and prisons,
Japanese   2. World War, 1939–1945——Personal
narratives   3. Burma–Siam Railway
  I. Title
  940.54'72'520924   D805.J3

ISBN 0–551–01257–9

Typeset by Wyvern Typesetting Ltd, Bristol
Printed in Great Britain by
Hazell Watson & Viney Ltd,
Member of the BPCC Group,
Aylesbury, Bucks.

*This book is dedicated to the memory
of the many who died in South East Asia
whilst in captivity under the Japanese during World War 2.*

Acknowledgements

My sincere thanks are due to the Christian Churches, Fellowships, Associations, Missionary Societies, Evangelistic Committees and the FGBMFI who have provided information and given approval for mentions within this book.

My gratitude and thanks go also to Linda and Gordon for their invaluable work in editing and typing the entire manuscript.

Not least of all, I am thankful to my wife Agnes, who has been an inspiration and support so necessary in one's Christian life.

This story is factual, but some fictitious names have been used.

Foreword

It is a great pleasure to me to write these words of introduction to this book which has been written by my friend Andy Milliken. I have known Andy for over twenty years and was particularly pleased to hear that he was going to write a book about his experiences, both in war and peace. Over the years, I have met a number of the men who were prisoners of war of the Japanese and were involved in building the notorious railway in Thailand. A number of these men became Christians during their period of hardship while others became Christians subsequently. I, too, have been intrigued to meet Japanese Christians who have gone through a similar experience since the war. I am sure this book is going to be an encouragement to many who have doubts about the faithfulness of God. Andy has been a man of faith in many spheres of ministry. I think this book will speak for itself and will help young and old alike to recognise the hand of God in the life of a man who has allowed that life to be fashioned by God Himself. I recommend this book and trust that it will be read by many people who will find its fascinating story a means of strengthening their own faith.

Canon Michael Harper
August 1984

Preface

Had it not been for a small book, a praying mother and an unexpected encounter with a nursing sister, this book might never have been written. During recent years, despite numerous requests from friends and colleagues, I have found many excuses for not sitting down and putting pen to paper. An opportunity finally presented itself in the form of unexpected redundancy, resulting in ample time to prepare a personal testimony. With one aim in mind: that of sharing a dependence upon the scriptures which, through these forty years, has become a living word within my life, I began to write. Little has been heard of those who were engaged in the war in South East Asia, particularly the thousands who were captured in the Far East during 1942–1945. It would probably be correct to say that it was not until some fifteen years after the dropping of the bombs of Nagasaki and Hiroshima that a name, now synonymous with the Far East, began to emerge: the Kwai. This book records a testimony from personal experience. It shows how God can reach and deliver any one of His choosing and bring hope and light to those in times of darkness and despair through His word, under the anointing of the Holy Spirit. While there is a desire to encourage the reader, this book does little to minimise the brutality and appalling conditions suffered by the thousands who never returned. Today, one can see a sad memorial to all who died building the railway at the War Graves Cemetery in Kanchanaburie although the holiday brochures advertise an 'enjoyable' trip up the famous

Kwai, visiting the Bridge, with many local Thais evidently making the most of the publicity engendered within the last twenty years.

Through the forty years since the war I have never ceased to be amazed at the remarkable way in which God has gone before in almost every situation, in both home and business life. I am thankful for having been able to take part in the Greater London Crusade of 1954 and also witness the outpouring of the Holy Spirit in Fleet Street showing how God can use Christians in the commercial world of publicity. In every situation I have recognised how the scriptures can become the Living Word in one's own life.

I am constantly reminded of those three and a half years in captivity and how I came to know, with firm assurance, a complete dependence upon the Word of God. I recall, with a thankful heart, the way Jesus has never failed or let me down and has kept His promises ever since that first encounter in the far off jungle camp along the banks of the River Kwai.

1: The Rising Sun Over South East Asia

'PEARL HARBOUR ATTACKED . . .!' the shattering announcement resounded over the ship's public address system, breaking the morning calm on the crowded decks during that unforgettable day, 7th December 1941. At 7.49 a.m. that morning, Captain Mitsuo Fuchida, Commander of the Japanese task force, had shouted the command 'Zengun Totsugeki Seyo' – 'Let's go' and 360 aircraft had roared into action. Japan was at war. As our American flagship sailed in convoy, somewhere off the west coast of South Africa, little did we realise how that assault was to affect our lives for the next four years.

Some weeks earlier, our Division had embarked on a number of American transports at Halifax, Nova Scotia, after a rather stormy voyage across the North Atlantic in a well-used Polish ship from Gourock, near Glasgow. Being aboard the converted luxury liner of the American fleet gave us a fair idea of peacetime cruising as we sailed through the colourful Caribbean. Flying fish and dolphins crossed and recrossed in front of the huge bulk of the 33,000 ton vessel.

Once the news was out, Pearl Harbour was naturally the main topic of the day. The whole war situation as it was in Europe, together with this cowardly attack, brought little encouragement to any of us on board. As I pondered these events, little did I imagine that the day would come, many years after the war, when I would come face to face with

Captain Fuchida in England.

A few days later, the convoy, which had zig-zagged its way across the Southern Atlantic within the shelter of the South American continent, having changed course, was now sailing towards Cape Town. The familiar silhouette of Table Mountain was etched against the deep red morning sky as we steadily made our way towards the port of Cape Town. It was a welcome change to set our feet on the South African soil after several weeks on one of the great oceans of the world.

During the few days of our stay, we met with a warm welcome from the locals with their large limousines collecting and escorting many of the crew around the beautiful suburbs and shorelines of the Table Bay area. The deep azure sea, lined with large white crested waves, provided an unexpected opportunity for surfing. The days were rewarding and relaxing, although we noticed with unease that most of the urban trains and buses clearly indicated divisions for 'Whites' and 'Blacks'. During the Cape Town shore leave, mail from home was distributed, and we replied to loved ones, knowing it might be our final few words before battle.

We got used to the idea that with Japan in the war America would have to engage with the Japanese in the Pacific. As we weighed anchor our thoughts drifted to our likely destination: we were trained for desert warfare, which meant we would be making our way round the Cape and up the east coast of Africa to either the Red Sea or Persian Gulf.

The following week our journey was interrupted by two events. The convoy split up with most of the ships sailing on, but we veered to the portside, sailing in the opposite direction, going west. On the horizon land was just visible, which gradually enlarged into an entire palm tree lined coast. As we progressed towards the coast, wondering whether we would dock, a narrow channel came into view lined with coconut trees. The ship's company took soundings as they carefully sailed into this natural approach and eventually into a wider, busy seaport harbour. It was Mombassa. The fact that we were only four degrees south of the Equator was soon evident when the ship's massive engines ceased to vibrate. Immediately, the cooling breeze was cut off and amid the onslaught of the tropical heat the anchors were lowered. As with all new ports, most of us were eager to explore the town which was full of dark skinned natives decoratively dressed in a variety of patchwork materials vibrantly coloured. Very soon swarms of mosquitos invaded the ship's sleeping quarters, making constant swatting during the early evening more than necessary prior to 'brown-out'.

Later in the week the sound of the anchors being hauled out of the water brought a sigh of relief from us all, and the local tug boats came alongside for the careful manoeuvring of our huge vessel for the turnround, ready for sailing. Immediately the engines commenced, the breeze returned, and we sailed out through the narrow channel to be met by a cloudless sky and the sun's shimmering reflection across the open sea; the air was refreshing. Beyond the palm-lined reef, eagerly looking for an opportunity to boast of our rather mediocre navigational expertise, we kept a constant watch in the direction we were sailing. Several days elapsed and it became evident that we were not going anywhere near the Red Sea – but were sailing east! One delightful event broke the monotony of our surroundings. We approached a beautiful atoll, where we anchored for a day to take on water and diesel. Only the supply vessel spoiled this idyllic south-sea island setting which we were to recall in the gloom of the years to come. As we peered over the ship's side, we were able to see right to the bottom and see the silvery sand dotted with numerous strange looking marine creatures.

There was little doubt where we were destined – Singapore. We had a vague idea where it was located; somewhere near China was the best suggestion! With the swiftness of the Japanese attack, Hong Kong seemed in imminent danger of falling; the Philippines and numerous other islands of the Pacific were also under threat. The following days were spent familiarising ourselves with the terrain in the Federal Malay States, what the jungle would be like for warfare and survival, and the type of enemy we might face – the Japanese warrior. The previous 'brown-outs' after sun down were now changed to 'black-outs', more in keeping with those back at home in the United Kingdom. On several occasions enemy alerts were sounded, but fortunately with no sign of the Japanese, either in the air, on, or under the sea. The American naval personnel soon changed to wearing full combat dress when on station duty. Regular interest in the latest news bulletins, now not only concerned us, but also the Americans. By this time the enemy was fighting in Indo-China, Hong Kong, China, Thailand and was entering parts of Malaya. Several naval battles were reported in the South China Seas. With the speed of these spearheads into South East Asia we began to wonder who would arrive first at Singapore. One night we at last reached Sunda Straits, dividing Java and Sumatra, and within two days had arrived at Singapore.

Early on that January morning in 1942 we sailed into the Naval Docks on the north east side of Singapore Island. Little did we think that on that morning, whilst complaining of the heavy monsoon which lasted most of the day, the Lord already had His hand upon us. Every morning at

16

10.00 local time, a formation of Japanese fighter bombers would arrive and pattern-bomb highly populated areas of Malayan towns. Had the usual morning sunshine been in evidence that day, our ship would have been a prime target.

The first night in Singapore was far different from the enticingly exotic views advertised in the holiday brochures of today. Under canvas, in pouring rain, the flow of water running through most of the tents, we sat on our kit bags hoping for a respite. For the first and only time in my somewhat chequered military career I found myself enjoying a drink of hot cocoa laced with a large tot of rum. Immediately after arriving in Singapore, our Brigade was despatched across the lengthy causeway linking the island with the state of Johore Bahru. The days that followed consisted of fierce and heavy fighting in and around Ayer Hitam, Yong Peng and Pontain Kechil.

It is hard to forget the terrorist tactics of the ambushes by well trained jungle fighters of the Japanese forces throughout the Malayan campaign as the bitter war continued. The following week, further convoys arrived, including the one which originally separated from us when approaching Mombassa. Strategic withdrawals from the mainland back to Singapore occurred, and on 3rd February the Causeway was blown up by the Royal Engineers, leaving us an island in every sense of the word. The Japanese soon became known for their vicious attacks: skilfully camouflaged with Tamil and Malaysian drapery to cover their true identity as many moved in the tree tops of the jungle. Discharging hand grenades from tree tops, firecrackers in other places, they caused panic amongst the Chinese and Indians in Singapore. Friday 13th February will never be forgotten, with the enemy attacking on all fronts, armed with heavy artillery, mortar and aircraft bombardment, and the long range guns from the Naval units out beyond Singapore Island. One morning a pattern formation attack caught many of us out in the open near the Nee Soon district of Singapore, and, looking up at twenty five menacing aircraft droning in strike formation towards us, thunderous ack-ack fire blasted our ears as we all dived for cover, some into malarial drains, others into small ditches, and two of us beneath an army vehicle for protection against shrapnel.

Seconds later, as a salvo of high explosives hit the ground nearby, our bodies were lifted by the vibration. The bombs fell about a quarter of a mile away. After the all-clear we scrambled out from our shelter to be met by a Corporal who sarcastically informed us the lorry we had sheltered under contained high explosives!

The Japanese air offensives were perfectly co-ordinated, either with the twin engine fighter bombers at high level or with zero type dive bombers used on many low level sorties. As records have since confirmed, air support to our services was very limited.

By now Singapore was a blazing inferno. A huge black swirling cloud issued from the oil containers and climbed high into the sky forming a long black trail out to sea.

The Japanese had crossed the swamp lands of west Singapore and into the reservoir areas near Bukit Timah and, with ammunition dumps being captured or blown up, the civilians in Singapore were in a very difficult situation as the British and Australian troops were forced back in a circle outside Singapore city.

The Japanese then demanded total surrender of the British: February 14th was a demoralising day for us all. The heat was fearful – so was the smell of death. There was complete devastation: both Indian and Chinese, mostly civilians, lay rotting in the roadways. Lamp posts, telegraph poles, palm trees, were uprooted. Wires and electric cables trailed pathetically over the gaping shells of the bombed houses. It was the end of Singapore.

2: Captivity with a Little Book

SURRENDER . . . this was the word echoing around Singapore the next day, February 15th 1942. For British, Australian, Indian, Chinese and Asiatics alike, it had taken place at the Ford Motor Works on the Bukit Timah Road. The ceasefire was issued for 10.00 pm and it was estimated around 60,000 men were involved.

That evening the sky was filled with cascading rockets, flares and flames from buildings still burning after the attacks of the previous day. Dark clouds filled the skies, tinged with a deep crimson reflection from the devastation below: it was a pitiful sight. For many, it was the first opportunity to snatch a few hours of much needed sleep since the outbreak of hostilities.

As dawn appeared to bring to an end what seemed a very bad dream, it also brought an end to our freedom, a gift that is rarely appreciated until it is lost. During the next few days we experienced continual roll calls, check ups and uncertainty as we saw the first of our captors – small in stature, rugged, and far from considerate. A movement order came three days after the surrender and on 18th February we embarked on a fifteen mile trek, with full kit, towards the eastern area of Singapore Island. The sun in its zenith made the march, which started at noon, almost unbearable. As we set off along the Sarangoon Road, through the numerous ruined villages, the Japanese flag dominated the landscape. The 'rising sun' taunted us with every exhausting step.

Our destination was Changi, near the infamous jail, where it took only a week to settle in to a routine. If nothing else, the British have determined resilience which enables them to adapt under extreme conditions. The civilians were separated from us and were interned in the city jail for most of their three and a half years as prisoners. The overall conditions were far from comfortable, although for the first few weeks the Japanese required little work to be done.

Food became very precious. At first we were selective but we were quick to realise that survival was the all important factor and that we had to make the most of all available resources. Once the tea stocks had dwindled, our diet consisted of unpolished rice washed down with boiling water.

Occasionally we would be ordered on a working party, which meant about fifty of us would be transported by open lorry, each clutching the other to prevent falling on to the roadside. The day out to the dockyard always made an interesting change although it involved loading or unloading Japanese ships which often included ammunition and weapons.

The Japanese sought as much publicity as they could get. Their big day was when they arranged for all the prisoners taken at Singapore to be lined up on both sides of the Changi–Singapore road. Several of the high Military Officials drove down the road in convoy surveying us with immense satisfaction, as numerous camera crews followed taking motion pictures for their archives. This episode, on the so-called 'Road to Singapore', provided the first opportunity since the fall of Singapore to meet some of our friends in other British units. The Japanese wanted to boast of their Greater Asia Co-prosperity Sphere Campaign, and issued us with free copies of the new *Straits*

Times of Singapore.

During these months, there were times when I was presented with many tough encounters. I would quietly pray to God for help; so far as I was concerned it did not seem to come! Now I was only one of 60,000 prisoners and probably forgotten by many back home. During our leisure time in the camp at Changi most of the men had some kind of literature to read, whether it was a novel, newspaper, magazine or even a dictionary; it helped pass the time away. I had none of these, only a gift from my mother when I entered the Services: a little book not more than four inches by three, containing around 600 pages and in eye-straining small print. My father had carried this small book throughout his time in the Services during World War 1, and since I had received it from my mother it had remained at the bottom of my kit bag. I began to read it. After all I had nothing else to read, so why not? I ignored others in the camp who wondered why I was taking an interest in such a small book. When you thought about religion or christianity you were either Church of England or Roman Catholic, anything else was suspect. But what of my C. of E. identity tag around my neck under my regimental number? After all, I did go to the church in Walthamstow regularly every Sunday night! It did not mean much to me, but I did go, and was a Christian as far as I was concerned. There had been times when I had heard the Good News and failed to respond to it; but nothing fails to catch the all seeing eyes and ears of the Lord. During the next three years it was strange how the Lord began to work on me: He will certainly go to great lengths to obtain a captive audience! God allowed me to travel over 10,000 miles. Fortunately for us He never lets us go beyond the circle of His love. Although we are sometimes thoughtless He is anxious that none should

22

perish in this world. In keeping with an inner conviction due to my church background, I well remember attending a Communion Service, arranged because of a visit by the Bishop of Singapore. It was held in an attractively built bamboo open hut within the camp confines. For many years during his life, the Bishop was able to give outstanding testimonies of courage shown as a prisoner. At the time of my capture, I was unaware that two churches in the Walthamstow area, as well as my mother, were praying for me. Forty years on I now know that when anyone prays, however impossible the situation may seem, there is always a reply from God: with Him nothing is impossible. The little book, which was to be my source of encouragement for the coming years, was like a delayed-action bomb: it held the key to all my problems, although I did not realise it at the time, and thankfully I continued to read it nearly every day.

Several months had passed, with little in the way of news, when a special detail was called by the Japanese that several of our groups were to prepare for moving the next day. One's kit was now precious, but, as we found when we had to transport everything ourselves, any superfluous items soon had to be abandoned. Starting out from Changi many lads carried unbelievable items of kit; it was ironic that in later months many could barely carry themselves and their scanty clothing of scraps of sacking.

A twenty-two mile march faced us the following day, along the Changi Road through parts of Singapore city and out towards the north west passing Bukit Timah, to a new camp. This was to be our base for the next five months and, in retrospect, it was by far the best of any of our camps during captivity. We were detailed to various huts and we eagerly climbed up the wooden steps, thankful for the raised accommodation, since scorpions, centipedes and sometimes snakes were prevalent. Each of us claimed a particular corner or space, dropped our kit bag and mopped our sweaty brows after the gruelling forced march which we had continued during the daylight hours of intense sunshine. As I swept away the dust to clear a space for my kit I picked up an old school file to mark out my 'territory'. To my amazement the crest on the cover belonged to the Technical College I had attended in Walthamstow; how it had ever been brought to Bukit Timah in Singapore, and by whom, I will never know. Thoughts of home filled my mind: many a time we would sit back reminiscing of our homes and families until someone threw something in our direction and we were brought back to reality with a jolt. The Technical College, leaving school, working on my first job in Shoe Lane, hoping to be a compositor in the newspaper industry, changing in mid-stream and starting in an advertising agency in High Holborn – all this flashed through my mind.

How had I landed up in Bukit Timah, holding the school file with no scholar's name on it? I recalled saying farewell to my mother, another experience I found hard, as I walked off down the road in civilian clothes for the last time, until the end of the war. . . .

I recalled our first staging post after several hours journey on our special train. It was the Drill Hall in the cattle market area of Norwich. Here I enlisted and was given a number, as I entered the military services of the Royal Corps of Signals. The following weeks, as we endeavoured to become soldiers, were punctuated with many amusing episodes: it was just as well we were hidden in the countryside of Suffolk not many miles from Diss. Fleet Street cartoonists would have had a field day had they seen the office workers, journalists, artists and teachers within our Signal Corps, trying their best, or at least, trying the Sergeant Major's patience, in the country lanes during the drill instructions.

The first morning, we had what, at first, seemed to be an excellent idea – a cross country run before breakfast; however, our enthusiasm faded after we had only completed a quarter of the circuit. Most of us were well and truly out of condition and found that first morning the most strenuous and demoralizing experience of our lives. Eventually we staggered into the camp, noting as we passed the N.C.O's mess tent, the Physical Training Sergeant finishing a hearty breakfast – dressed in his best parade uniform. Would we ever make the grade? The first evening out saw most of us making for the one and only telephone kiosk in the village to call our homes back in London. I, like most of the others, shared the fear that if this was the first day, what of the future? I suppose this would have been the day most of us would have chosen, given the opportunity, to run back to mother quickly! The training we later realised was for our own good.

The main street in a village near Botesdale must have been the scene of entertainment for the locals, peering out of their cottage windows, as, one day, a unique performance was given by the so-called 'conscripts'. Drilling by the Sergeant Major was very definite and exacting, but for some reason I doubt whether he was getting much co-operation from us as we stared, open-mouthed, at his gesticulating and somewhat strange language. He descended to his knees and did something I have never seen an N.C.O. do ever again . . . he cried out in no uncertain terms . . . 'Oh, God, please send me some soldiers!' Not a very encouraging prayer. We were doing our best. I suppose his prayer was answered, for we were not discharged from the services until many years later.

25

Discipline was rapidly drummed into us even on the first night when we were informed by a small, yet very tough Corporal, that it was lights out. Then he switched off the lights, slammed the door and visited other rooms filled with noisy occupants. One of our number got out of his bunk and conveniently switched the lights on again for us all to read a few more chapters or write a few more lines. The return visit of that N.C.O. some ten minutes later, provided such a shock reaction that few publishers would consider printing his rapid-fire adjectives, some of which were new to me. Lights out became a very sacred thing after that.

Training in the Royal Corps of Signals was very interesting especially the telecommunications, radio and other methods of signalling. We had a good team spirit throughout the period of our service career.

Leaving the Norfolk area, we spent the winter in the Tweed Valley, followed by a few months in Cheshire prior to preparing for embarkation from Glasgow.

After all these lighthearted and precious daydreams, which we often shared with one another, it was with reluctance that we came down to earth again, always wondering why we 60,000 had finished up prisoners of the Japanese Imperial Army.

3: Jungle Bound for Thailand

The purpose of our stay in the Bukit Timah camp was to work on the new layout and construction of a Shinto shrine near the MacRitchie Reservoir, which meant the demolition of the pre-war golf course and changes to the nearby waterways. Although most of us were classified as Church of England, few liked the idea of helping to build a shrine – but then we had little choice in the matter.

Guards were rarely seen in our camp. Food was probably the best we would ever receive and we had a Yasume (rest day) once a week. This day was devoted to all personal maintenance, ablutions, church service and a concert. Within our ranks we had the ambitious and the resourceful; those who managed to escape camp without getting caught by Japanese patrol units and barter some of our worldly possessions with the natives in exchange for more important items, such as food.

Rumours of persuasive measures by the Japanese in the Changi area to obtain the signature of each prisoner to 'a no-escape promise form' reached our camps. Eventually we were requested to comply with this commitment. The first reaction in the Selerang Barrack area of Changi resulted in all prisoners being forced into the open, in a confined space, with kit, utensils and food, until the forms were signed. The British held their ground until the Japanese started making moves to get all the sick and wounded out of the hospital. There was no alternative but to sign.

By the end of October 1942, activity and interest grew as rumours reached us of the first International Red Cross shipment which had docked in Singapore from Portuguese East Africa. We were each issued with a soft hat, shirt, pair of shorts, some packets of cigarettes and boiled sweets – my quota of sweets increased as I found a good exchange rate for my cigarette ration. Bulk supplies in the form of medical equipment and drugs were much appreciated and in great demand by the hospital units. Forms of malt, sugar, team milk, fruit, corned beef, flour and chocolate were a welcome sight in the cookhouse. It was the only gift that many of us would receive for years to come.

Within a few days, following a Japanese inspection, our camp was under instructions to move and we were soon marching five miles to the edge of the city, once again with full kit, the Japanese allowing us three short breaks en route. Recovering from the blistering heat, we were paraded into the main Singapore Railway Station. Rumours of our destination soon flew around and although they were mostly unfounded they always provided interest and speculation. If we were to go by train there were some alluring destinations in Malaya and many were considered as a potential panacea for the prisoners. However, as we climbed the cattle trucks, the Japanese pushing about thirty of us into each one, with kit and cooking utensils, any thoughts of a rest cure were soon dispelled. The narrow gauge of the Federal Malay States Railway made the area of our truck appear much smaller than it really was. It took several minutes for each of us to get settled on the wooden floor; a mass of arms and legs were interwoven to achieve maximum stretching space. With the doors slammed tight, the train gave a jolt, after which we began to steam out of the station on our way north. Through the cracks in the side of the truck we could determine the terrain through which our train was heading – over the Causeway once again, into Johore Bahru, we set off on a journey which was to be a one way trip. For the first few hours on that warm afternoon we did not realise that our accommodation for the next few days would be far from comfortable.

During the day the steel trucks held the heat like massive boilers, and with the low night temperatures it was bitterly cold. The train made its way through each of the Malaysian States penetrating some of the thickest jungle in the world, the continuous shrieking siren echoing in the valley in true American style, as we passed northward over numerous wooden bridges. By night the powerful searchlight on the front of the engine stabbed into the darkness of the dense jungle which surrounded us. Each day we halted at a wayside junction to take on fuel and water, this being the only time we were able to stretch our legs. Getting out of the train for only a few moments was a great relief to each of us, as it was the only way to change position during the long day and night travel. I am sure Kuala Lumpur was never the same as when we queued up by the large water tank to get the overflow from the pipe – our wash for that week. The platforms were crowded with Malays, Japanese and Chinese, all looking somewhat puzzled at numerous nude British prisoners of all shapes and sizes revelling in the cooling water for the last few minutes that remained before moving on.

During our stops we could see that our train consisted of nearly thirty wagons. At the beginning of our journey we were hauled by the old Federal Malay State Railways engine as far as Ipoh, after which a Thai State locomotive took over. We travelled through Penang and Alor Star, and on through the Perak Mountains where the gradients were so steep that three locomotives were engaged to overcome the mountainous regions. Five days later our train pulled into a little village called Ban Pong; we were in Siam, now known as Thailand, which means the 'Land of the Free'. The previous day, when we halted for fuel, we had noticed many natives by the railside all eager to obtain anything we possessed. The majority were looking for a way to make a 'fast buck'.

It was now October 26th and we were met by excited Japanese soldiers desperately trying to count how many prisoners they were supposed to have in their possession. We spent one night in a dismal bamboo hut. The bamboo slats for the bedding were about two feet off the ground, which was fortunate for us as the entire camp hut area was under a foot of murky water from the recent monsoons. Any ideas of a rest cure were eliminated from our thoughts as we tried to sleep through night temperatures of 30°F or lower. Eagerly we awaited the sun, which broke through quickly after the dawn sounds of the jungle nearby. The heat could be felt just after nine and we soon dried out.

Food in this camp was far from good, with weed-like stew and continual swarms of large black flies ready to settle on every bite. Each time a guard came anywhere near us we all had to get up, and make a fairly curt bow, unless we wanted to be struck down for insolence. This, and numerous other demoralising requirements, caused us to consider what one author has since written, that we were merely 'the white coolie'. As we collected our kit that morning we thought the situation could not be worse, but how wrong we were. This new country was so different from Singapore Island, which, whilst very hot, always had a gentle refreshing breeze blowing across the country areas. Thailand gave us that heavy feeling of sticky heat, without a breath of fresh air anywhere. For the next few weeks, we were continually thirsty but had to remember that if we wanted to survive, we could only drink liquids which had been boiled thoroughly. We were in territory where cholera, bubonic plague, dysentery, malaria and black water fever, to name but a few, were prevalent, not forgetting the insects and predators. Fortunately the Japanese were as fearful of these diseases as we were and made sure most of us were given the necessary inoculations by their medical orderlies.

Ban Pong, situated about eighty miles west of Bangkok, the capital and Oriental city of Thailand, was to become the important junction and staging area for a new railroad linking Rangoon with Bangkok and Singapore by way of Moulmein, Thanbyuzayat and Ban Pong. The British and Allied prisoners would be instrumental in supplying the missing link on the two hundred and fifty miles of track through exceedingly treacherous and hostile country, where, in some parts, white man had never ventured. Those with a fair knowledge of geography and geology acquainted us with the region: malarial swamps, poisonous bamboo trees, steep rugged mountains with continuous downpours during the monsoon – our task seemed impossible.

Our mode of transport changed from steel trucks to old American lorries, and it was fifty of us, at least, per lorry, with full kit. Most of the fifty mile journey was experienced with us all in a standing position desperately gripping each other to prevent falling as the Japanese driver reached speeds of 45 mph along the pot-holed dirt track which passed as a road. Most of the journey was across flat plains with paddy fields and palm oil trees.

First we headed towards a strange town – Kanchanaburie. We did not stop, but continued through the one and only street, reminiscent of the Mid-Western

States ghost towns: I caught sight of a large Buddhist Temple with its weathered gold decor on the pointed flames on the edge of the roof. Our Japanese driver, intent on getting us to our destination, swung round several bends onto an open expanse revealing the large snake-like bend of a green river. Two large tributaries merged at this point in the bend of the river, one coming from the west, the larger from the north: the latter was the one alongside which our dusty roadway continued towards our presumed destination. Two miles on we drove into a large compound, with a clearing already prepared, to allow for more bamboo huts. There were already about five very long bamboo and atap leaf huts built by an advance party.

The camp, our new home, was surrounded by a line of irregular hills sweeping from the north where mountains outlined the horizon. Outside the camp were several rows of bamboo trees. We could not see the river but could just make out several steep mountains stabbing the skies away to the north west. This was presumably the intended direction for the future. The name of the camp was Tahmarkan; we did not realise then that this area was to be the site for a film which, years after the war, was to win many awards – *The Bridge on the River Kwai*.

4: Into the Valley of Death

Tahmarkan, cleared of much jungle vegetation for our camp, housed hundreds of prisoners in the next few weeks in preparation for building the notorious 'Railroad of Death', during the following year. Accommodation was fairly cramped: for the sake of both health and peace we each slept head to foot the whole length of the hut. Once the wheels were in motion our electricians managed to supply lighting to all our huts. In the cookhouse, catering was now on a larger scale and huge Indian kualis, metal saucer shape open bowls, were used to cook the rice: the water was boiled in disused petrol drums. Rations were meagre for the first few weeks but increased later. Our daily diet consisted of 24 ounces of rice (which had to last three meals), the occasional vegetable and very rarely, meat, the origin of which was anyone's guess!

Despite only a bamboo fence surrounding the camp, escape was near impossible. To the north-west lay nearly 1,000 miles of jungle, to the north and east swamps and mountains and, if that was not a deterrent, our give-away pale skin made us easy prey for native bounty hunters.

We noticed most of the guards in this area were much taller, and soon learned the reason. They were Koreans, also under the heel of the Japanese, and therefore even more brutal with their punishments. A large guard room was situated at the main entrance where guards were on 24 hour duty. Our main concern was not the guards but the survival of the lads in the camps, to remain united, appreciating we were all in the same predicament. There have been many stories of feuds amongst prisoners on other islands in the Pacific, but I knew of no such disagreements in any of the camps we were in; the lads rallied together and the morale was good considering the strenuous circumstances that lay ahead.

Following the roll call, or Tenko as it is known by the Japanese, we marched in column past the guard room, along the bamboo trees until we caught first sight of the project. We came to a long sloping embankment which led to the river. A partially constructed wooden bridge spanned the murky water and we noticed a fleet of transport craft manned by dwarf-like Thais, chewing betelnut whilst waiting for us. The river was fast flowing from the north and swollen following the recent monsoons. According to our map this was the River Kwai Noi, part of the Mekhlong River. The sight before us was the same that captured the imagination and inspiration of the film makers.

There were to be two bridges, the initial wooden one providing immediate transportation while the large bridge, which comprised around twelve spans made of concrete and iron girders, was under construction. The wooden bridge also acted as a standby in the event of Allied attacks on the other bridge. Once the bridge was complete, it was within range of the Liberator bombers from Allied held territory, and was bombed a number of times. Sabotaging the bridge during construction was uppermost in our minds but we had little chance of succeeding due to Japanese engineers continually overseeing our work.

Directly across the bridge we noticed a hive of activity, for here a pathway was under construction. A party was engaged in cutting back the dense undergrowth and the notorious bamboo trees: a scratch to the skin would invariably result in poisoning. A tool known as a chunkle, similar to a large hoe, was issued to everyone and its use soon became apparent. The pathway on the far bank quickly took shape and signalled the start of excavation along the route, whereupon a human conveyor belt shifted basket loads of soil to the top of the pathway. To break the monotony and thus maintain our sanity we teamed up with a colleague for the day. We discussed every conceivable topic. I recall naming most of the stations on the Piccadilly Line from Cockfosters to Acton Town, or the names of all the pubs, cinemas and churches one would pass on a number eleven bus from Liverpool Street to Victoria! When we had completely dried up of things to talk about we would change partners.

With Service personnel, volunteering can have some amusing connotations, as it did during the start of the building of the large bridge across the Kwai. The call had gone out the previous evening for volunteers for an interesting job the following day. I, with several others, decided a change was as good as a rest; after all, we had to work which ever way we looked at it. Our select party formed after roll call and we smartly made our way following a small Japanese guard, feeling fairly confident we were on to something pretty good as we left the main groups setting off to other areas. We were spread out in pairs along the rivers edge up the sloping boards to the height of the level for the large bridge. From nine am we started the now familiar conveyor system of passing baskets loaded with ballast, rubble and sand. By now our quiz games were not as interesting or novel as before! At nine pm we were still passing baskets full of rubble; midnight came and went and we were still working. Finally, at about three am, we were allowed to crawl back to our bunks after nearly eighteen hours shift, but in all fairness to the Japanese 'shop steward', we had a five minute break every two hours with half an hour lunch and dinner break. We never did find the person responsible for putting forward our names for that 'voluntary' work. From that day on we were always backward in coming forward.

The bridge was now taking shape; the huge concrete structures were reaching the required level. Steel girders were transported from a bridge in Java and under the direction of Japanese engineers, we had the daunting task of ensuring they were positioned correctly. Another working party was engaged on what was known as pile driving; ten or twelve men, each holding a rope attached to a main cable where a heavy iron weight was precariously balanced over a long teak bulk log. On the count of three everyone pulled their rope then simultaneously released them, ensuring they were well clear when the weight came pounding down to the ground.

Close by was Chungkai camp, later to become well known, and each day we would meet many of the prisoners from that camp along the roadway. We would join forces in the day-to-day activity of embankment structure, ballast support, chunkling, or digging.

One day, as we dug deeply into the ground around some tree roots, we dislodged a nest of scorpions. I had never seen any so large, seven or eight inches wide across the claws and up to ten inches with the tail extended. We immediately prodded these horrific black creatures on the back with our tools, hoping to see self infliction of their deadly sting, like in the text books. Even in our huts, before we ever put on our clothes, we had to check that no foreign body was lurking. The Malaysian centipedes are giants compared with our common or garden species.

Almost seven inches long, their dark brown shell measures one and a half inches wide with, on each side, half inch long poisonous feet which would scratch deep into human flesh if one inadvertently brushed the centipede downwards instead of flicking it up and away from the skin. Cobras and pythons were often seen near our camp also, as were numerous smaller varieties of unwelcome reptiles.

The bridge was now nearing completion and, simultaneously, the track had been laid from Ban Pong, as it was now being layed from the bridge to Chungkai and further north. Several times we were given the task of carrying heavy teak sleepers. This usually needed three men but if they were of different heights, the brutal weight, especially when we had to cross a ditch, was unbearable. It was the same when we were detailed to carry the track, sacks on our shoulders acting as protection from the rusty rail which dug deep into our skin. Many backs today still bear the scars of those heavy rails, where grazed shoulders, mingled with blood, sweat and dirty sacking, caused agonising pain before eventual healing.

A desperate move by the Japanese to complete the entire railway was put into motion: they called it 'speedo' and meant every word of it. Every few miles beyond Chungkai, Tarsoa, Kinsyok, and further north west, camps were full of hundreds of our men falling sick from countless diseases. Not only were the Japanese at their worst when battering our men, or forcing sick men from their beds to work when they should have been hospitalised, but the natural environment was also at its most hostile, with torrential monsoons, disease, bamboo, insects and vermin all aggravating our already poor health.

Horrific tales were filtering down through the railway from the camps near the Burma border. Cholera had broken out and with that swift death that so often followed within a day or two: many of the sufferers that were on working projects could hardly stand and had to be carried back at night, some to die only days later. Malaria and beri-beri also took their toll, as did dysentery and colic. No one was immune from the terrible shadow of death cast over the entire countries of Burma, Thailand and Malaya.

During this testing time, something happened to me in which I was severely hurt, but the Lord, as He had done before, had His hand upon me. On this particular morning I was acting 'teaboy' for the day; for once a lightweight job! Two of us spent the day gathering wood, filling a huge kerosene drum with water from the river and supplying adequate amounts of boiling water to drink. For months now, we had only the boiling water to drink; tea or coffee had long since been eliminated from our menu, although when thirsty it was still a delight to drink the boiling water from our mess tin, leaving a sediment of dusty soil. We were sited near to where most of the work was being carried out that day, a few of my mates taunting me on having obtained the tea job for the day. Just before lunchbreak as we were preparing the smaller pails ready for distribution to the lads, my partner was collecting the boiling water ready to pour into the pails when his container jolted the side of an oil drum and sent scalding water streaming down my leg. I could not recall if I cried, shouted, or just went blank. The pain was excruciating. Some of the lads grabbed handfuls of dirty grease from the bogey axles from a nearby rail car and smeared it over my scalded skin. With no shoes for protection I was unable to walk so I was yet another victim destined for the hospital. The first few days and nights were almost unbearable, particularly as my 'favourite' medical orderly came with tweezers in hand to peel off the blisters leaving a large mass of red-raw skin. The next week in hospital I heard that the remainder of our camp were drafted to hell-like camps in the north, many never to return. It was a blessing in disguise that I had ended up in hospital – the hand of God was surely upon me.

Over the next few months in hospital, I assisted the M.O. by sketching the varying and changing conditions of patients – especially those whose tropical ulcers from bamboo scratches were radically changing each day.

The tropical ulcers often resulted in amputations. The medical authorities throughout the POW camps have to be given the highest commendations for their unceasing attempts to help the men, even with the limited supplies they had in their possession. If you had bad toothache, for example, you had the choice of having the tooth out without any anaesthetic, or suffering in silence, as drugs were precious and had to be reserved for more important casualties.

The bridge camp was slowly receiving the remainder of the tragic numbers of casualties from the jungle, and we witnessed, for the first time, unimaginable sights – they were walking skeletons. The railway was now nearing completion, and it was reported that for every sleeper on the route to Moulmein, a life was lost. Immediate indignation from the British and Allied Commandants in the camps, was to very little avail. In a pathetic gesture by the Japanese, they moved the remaining sick back to base camps in Kanchanaburie, Tamuang, and Tahmarkan, but it was too late.

The fateful sight of a circling vulture usually signalled death: these terrible beasts would circle our camp often confirming another death was imminent. Once, the strain became unbearable as we witnessed a dozen of our men being buried in one day. The notes of the Last Post became a dreaded all-too-familiar sound, and unendurable for many hollow-eyed men wondering who it was this time, and if they were next. It was at times like these that we doubted the reason for our existence and wondered why there were wars, why your friends were dying and why we were unable to help them? Tom and Ron, both good friends, had died, such good men, the very best. Why? We needed to find relief in someone or something. My only rest was in reading my little Book, it comforted me, and in traumas like this, turned my thoughts to God.

With no mail from home for over eighteen months and little in the way of reliable news, those two churches in East London continued to pray for me and others. Whilst I was still failing to grasp the daily agonies, the Lord was aiming to grasp me, and in His time was going to cause me to consider His ways for myself.

With the return of many broken men from the camps, another movement order came which included me.

5: Trapped

A few days later our move took us out of the camp on board 'our railway' in a south easterly direction, which we thought was a hopeful sign. The journey was not as long as we had expected, for after joining the main line junction at Ban Pong we travelled east and our train stopped about three miles further on at a camp called Hnong Pladuk. This camp was out in the open countryside. We had left the hills far beyond Kanchanaburie and now only vast expanses of paddy fields mingled with coconut palms surrounded us. It was estimated the camp could hold 5,000 prisoners, housed in sixteen bamboo huts erected high on wooden platforms, ideal for the many sick men requiring rest and assistance. Before long Hnong Pladuk was seen to have its full complement of prisoners. The general opinion was that it was going to be a much better camp compared with those we had experienced previously.

We were again rostered for working parties and it soon became apparent how vulnerable we would be if Allied bombers decided to 'investigate' the area. Opposite the camp and across several railway tracks we found ourselves by the main marshalling and engineering huts for maintenance on locomotives. Immediately to our east flank was the radio station, with a large petrol dump only a quarter of a mile away. A battery of Bofors anti-aircraft guns, manned by Indians under Japanese instruction, was situated at the rear of our camp, with a large Japanese transit camp neatly sited to our west. In fact, the entire POW camp was strategically sited in the centre of the would-be bombing targets, surrounded by a ditch, twenty five feet deep by fifty feet wide, with machine gun posts at each corner. Between the camp and Ban Pong lay an important freight depot, marshalling weapons and supplies up into the jungle during the dark of night.

It was now 1944, and many in the camp settled down to regular activities such as sports, training courses similar to Open University, concerts, church services and numerous other activities. The camp death toll was beginning to fall bringing with it new hope to us all. The medical officers and orderlies were now able to concentrate on getting the sick on a steady road to recovery. Many of our unit, who some months earlier were stationed in the jungle, were now back in Hnong Pladuk, and old friendships were renewed. I, like most, tried to keep a detailed diary, with the idea of leaving 'no stone unturned' in relating to our folks back home our experiences and our treatment by the Japanese. However, one morning, as we were sitting on our bamboo beds, writing, reading or just relaxing, the Japanese guards, led by the dreaded Kempeti, the secret police, burst into each hut demanding that everyone leave everything and prepare for roll call. There was little or no time to conceal anything. An hour went by: the sun beating down on us as we waited pensively on the parade ground. Many of us experienced mental terror as we wondered what would happen if any incriminating evidence, such as maps and reports would be discovered. Before long I was breaking out in a cold sweat as I remembered I had left my fully documented description of camp life, giving up to the minute detail, wide open for all to see. After about an hour the search ended: whatever they had been looking for was not evident. We hurried back to find our huts ransacked, beds turned upside down; even the bamboo slats had been ripped out. I thanked God that my diary was still lying undisturbed in exactly the place where I had hurriedly left it. That same day, after looking over the daily accounts in my diary, trying to memorise dates and events, I took the only course open to me if I was to avoid similar incidents with the Kempeti. Off I went to the latrines, diary in hand, and reluctantly disposed of it. With it went all the carefully written information that would have later proved so useful.

It was a beautiful, sunny June day; some were out on selective working parties, some in the workshops learning motor maintenance and others were on camp cleaning duties. We were half way through the year: how many more months or years would we have to endure before our release? It was nearly noon and the sun was almost overhead casting short shadows when several of us stopped what we were doing and listened, our ears straining: a familiar vibrating noise could be heard although few of us took much notice, especially the Japanese, but to those of us who heard, it was sweet music to our ears. It was an aircraft, and being so high it must be ours. As the noise from the engines grew louder, we were able to pick out an identifiable speck approximately 30,000 feet directly overhead. For at least ten minutes the aircraft maintained its interest in the area of Ban Pong and Hnong Pladuk. Where had it come from? The latest news to reach the camp was that the Americans and British must surely be on the way, but, as always, this was a rumour, since strategic information filtered through infrequently and only through a few brave men engaged in receiving newscasts, and risking their lives to do so.

During that night our ever inquisitive minds received a

sudden jolt at about two am. The moon was now on the wane, although on this peaceful night it was casting long shadows over the camp and the surrounding countryside. Suddenly we heard a very different sound of an aircraft, followed by screams from the gunners manning the anti-aircraft battery behind us. This aircraft was certainly much lower than the earlier one. It sounded heavy: it was approaching from the north west, and the alternating vibration of several engines indicated to us that it was on no joy ride. I and several others who had been sleeping in our quarters, were on our feet in a flash and rushed to the door of the hut craning our necks to catch a glimpse of what was making the noise. Others in the hut preferred to sleep on regardless. The several near misses I had experienced in the Singapore sorties had instilled in me a feeling of horror and fear at the prospect of being on the receiving end of yet another bombardment. As the plane crossed the camp and flew on east along the railway I breathed a sigh of relief. The plane was the source of great encouragement: it had not bombed us, and, as the ominous black shadow passed in front of the moon we at last began to feel that this was a turning point in the war and we would be on the winning side in the end. Within a few minutes though, we noted a distinct change in the tone of the engines. It was altering direction. It seemed to swoop in a half circle and then, as it was returning to our area, we thought it time to arouse the rest. We had no slit trenches to jump into as the Japanese had refused our application months ago. As we heard that familiar scream coming towards us, we all fell flat – motionless. Noise blasted out everywhere – guns, shouts, screams. The bombs were aimed at us – one crump, two crumps, each one getting louder with shuddering vibrations as the ground around us absorbed each blast. The next crump

44

seemed more distant unless we were imagining it, and the final onslaught had missed me and the men who were close by. By now, the full horror of the attack was evident, many running in anguish, others in a state of shock, whilst three of us, on hearing the sound of another bomber, decided to search for a safe refuge below ground: there was only one place we could think of – a small well. Although we wondered how deep it was or whether we should slide or jump in, we never had time to investigate properly – all three of us leapt in without a second thought as the next rush of heavy bombing started. Neck deep in murky water, we looked up and waited with bated breath. Bombs were exploding near the edge of the camp and again we observed those large black four-engined bombers circling. Fortunately for us, the main sidings of the Ban Pong train had been hit with pin-point accuracy. Explosions, followed by large bursts of flames, confirmed that the ammunition trucks had been hit. The unceasing roar of the heavy bombers must have continued for about half an hour. I cannot recall whether or not the Bofors guns continued. All I remembered later was, once again, calling to God, 'Please, please help me'.

Many were killed in that raid. Unfortunately, the Japanese, in their cunning, had placed us right in the target area hoping that because of us they would be safe from air attacks. How wrong they were! We could not blame the Allied air forces: they concentrated on the train the moment a plane scored a direct hit. In our camp, many soldiers of the Dutch East Indies attached to the Dutch forces appeared to have had little instruction on bomb drill, and evidently some were caught in the blast as they ran. On our return to the hut after seeing what assistance could be given, we found to our horror, that one man from our unit, who had decided to stay on his raised bed, had been badly wounded by flying shrapnel.

The next day an air raid warning was sounded by the Japanese, using a triangle iron at the guard room, as the faint but distinct noise of aircraft could be heard yet again. It was probably the same reconnaissance aircraft checking damage caused by the night raiders. With quick thinking on someone's part, a Union Jack, kept for military funerals, had been draped over one of the many corpses in the hope that when the photographs were examined they would take note of the casualties caused during their bombings. Whether this ploy worked, or if there was an undercover agent near Ban Pong who advised of the casualties, we shall never know, but we never heard another aircraft for many weeks.

Two months later things had got back to normal and the Japanese even allowed us to dig slit trenches. Working parties to the various local sites were underway. It was almost meal time and the sun was slipping towards the west on its last two hours of exposure on the dry lands of Thailand. As we were crossing the main line outside the camp the now familiar air raid alarm sounded: the chilling sound echoed out across the camp as we rushed back, making for the slit trenches near the huts. We waited, wondering if it was a false alarm, and hoping that we wouldn't be bombed again seeing we were prisoners of war. This faint hope soon dissolved into one of apprehension as we caught sight of nine silhouettes on the horizon: they appeared to be taking their time. This time they were coming from the east and the sun's rays caught parts of the formation resulting in sporadic flickering on the pilot's wind shields. However, this was no time for appreciating one of nature's phenomena, for these nine four-engined Liberators were making their way to the target with us in the middle. Every trench was crammed as we waited for what seemed an eternity: if only the Japanese would let us run, we thought, we could have run miles out across the paddy fields well away from the target area. What a frightening situation to be in when we knew the bombers were ours but could do nothing about it. Some of us preferred to keep our eyes on what we might expect to get or miss, and we watched the bomb bays open: they must have been no more than 10,000 feet above us. At that moment there appeared to be few atheists as all around me I heard cries to God for help. I too was afraid of the outcome. The moment they tipped their wings a series of black dots left the aircraft, as if in an effort to steer clear of our part of the target. All except one aircraft followed this pattern; it appeared that the bombs were released early, resulting in a salvo of blasts heading right for us. I cried out, 'God save me' – that cry, was to strike home again, in a time of trouble; I, like most, cried to God. It seemed that we always cried to God when we were in tight spots.

The familiar scream told us the heavy bombs were on their way. Everyone was crouched down with fingers in ears, eyes shut, and mouth open . . . waiting.

The tremendous explosions soon came. There was a blazing inferno as each of the nine planes' bombs exploded on the edge of our camp, along the sidings and across the marshalling yards. As I called to God, He heard me and delivered me right then! There were many casualties, but all around our part of the camp we had been saved from destruction – once again. I know that as the word of God says, 'Call unto Me and I will answer you, and show you great and mighty things' (Jer. 33.3) the only condition, for any who are in a tragic impossible situation, is you accept what God is saying and truly believe and hold onto His promise. The Holy Spirit will activate that promise and you will receive the answer. God says what He means, and all He wants you and me to do is believe it, and He does the rest. I called to God on that June day in 1944, and He heard and brought me through.

As far as I can recollect, a further wave of bombers came over from the south and repeated the raid, and finally we saw the formation turn and make their way towards the sun, now sinking in the west, returning to their base some hours away. Here in Thailand, God was certainly getting through to me, but it was to be some time before I fully appreciated how to respond to Him: I seemed to be learning the hard way. I knew that after this shattering experience, I had been saved and felt another step towards making it home to the UK.

Following this raid, uncertainty gripped the camp and increased as we heard many stories of those who had returned to Singapore from the jungle camps some months previously only to be lost in the South China Sea having been sunk by American submarines. More from our camp were being prepared to move, some to a hospital camp about twenty miles along the railway, others down to Malaya. It was my turn next.

6: From the Depths of Despair

It was rumoured that we had been selected for moving supplies for the Japanese. This time a number of prisoners were hand picked for duty which meant many from our original unit were separated. It was late afternoon as we boarded the open top waggons of the heavily loaded train outside the camp, praying that we would not be faced with Allied bombers looking for an easy target. However, we did not pull out till after the sun had slipped from the bright golden sky and night had descended. As we approached Ban Pong we anxiously waited to see which of the two lines we might be pushed on to: within minutes we realised we were not bound for the south and Singapore but, to our horror, we were on the jungle line again. As the rickety train chugged its way across the now familiar landscape towards Kanchanaburie, our thoughts were mixed with apprehension and a certain amount of fear – we were once again on the 'Railroad of Death'. Passing Kanchanaburie in the early evening, with its Buddhist temple overshadowing most of the town, we steamed on relentlessly until our train came round the curved approach to the Bridge over the Kwai. There slowed down almost to a halt, but the engine continued to shunt us onto the Bridge and we shuddered over the fast flowing river. There was little we could see in the dark of evening, but we sensed we were over the middle of a yawning chasm until the rumble changed as we reached the solid embankment on the far side. The train then began to accelerate as if it realised it had a long journey ahead. We recognised Chungkai on our left and, whilst we were thankful for the night movement, it was a decidedly uncomfortable ride. The train was fuelled mainly by timber and sparks continuously belched forth from the large funnel, showering the majority of the waggons. We spent the greater part of the journey ducking and diving in an attempt to avoid being hit by the red hot cinders.

Several days previously we had heard of terrifying air attacks on trains during daylight hours: as prisoners we had little chance of surviving such an attack.

Several hours elapsed and whilst we tried to keep our eyes and ears open to the dark night skies, we began to doze for a few moments, although there was a chance a stray Liberator bomber might just spot the sparks issuing from the locomotive. We were literally living on our nerves. We were soon woken from that brief moment of sleep by the siren on our locomotive suddenly screeching and echoing around the mountains as we approached, very slowly, a large viaduct. Dawn was breaking and we could make out our position, high up on the railway with about twenty double supports built around and under the cliff edge. The full height of the cliff must have been about five hundred feet above the track. Looking down from our waggon, which protruded precariously over the edge of the narrow gauge line, it seemed as though we were at least eight hundred feet above the raging river. We approached the bridge at a snail's pace not sure whether the driver had little faith in the construction of the bridge, or was giving a thrill to his passengers! Eventually the train made what appeared to be a winding double bend along the viaduct and once across, we then steamed into a dense teak forest with only a narrow clearing for the line which led us to another small wayside station, called Wampo. As I thought of the bridge itself, I could not help feeling it seemed an even bigger engineering feat than the bridge at Tahmarkan.

We disembarked and the party of about forty collected what kit we had and followed two guards. In our party, we had a senior NCO who was admirable in every way as he took charge and liaised with the Japanese on our behalf both then and for the next few months.

Leaving the hut-like station, we marched in single file through dense undergrowth, which, when cleared, provided us with commanding views over the terrain and the river. At this point the river's width was in the region of five hundred yards and coloured bottle-green. On the far banks bamboo trees overhung and partially concealed the water's edge. A boat awaited our party as we stumbled down the steep bank to the river and boarded this craft, flanked each end by the guards. Despite our circumstances, the sight across the river was so magnificent it almost distracted us from the fact that we were at war! Reaching the other side we were ushered up a steep path and, looking back the way we had come, there was now no sight of the railway – the natural camouflage concealed the line. Apparently the Japanese used this to their advantage throughout their Burma campaign. In a way we felt more secure now we were away from the line but how long this was to last was anyone's guess. A camp had been partially completed to house our party, as well as the Japanese, and we finished the accommodation in a day or two. We tried to piece together various bits of information, such as why so small a party and why the dirt track outside the camp trailed away to the west. We came up with various conclusions, none of which made much sense until a week later.

The project we were assigned to was to convert a small

footpath into a road wide enough to take handcarts initially and ultimately, lorries. The footpath led us along valleys, over large hills, which to us, carrying heavy sacks of food, seemed like mountains, down the slopes into more valleys and eventually, after many miles, into a staging post towards which, it was rumoured, a group of workers was making their way from the Tavoy direction. The first two months we assumed the role of packhorses, carrying stocks of food and equipment for the Japanese. The sacks were extremely heavy and had to be carried on several trips each week over the gruelling eight mile stretch. The first staging camp was appropriately named Chilly Valley. The high cliffs on each side blocked the direct sunlight and the only part of the camp to see any sun was the roofs to the huts, and that was only for an hour each day.

Nature can play havoc in the jungle, one minute it is enchanting, the next, extremely hostile. Several times we were in the middle of an electric storm, with sudden winds reaching hurricane force followed by tornado-like columns of black clouds. Ironically, our only place of refuge in these conditions, with trees being uprooted all around us, was our slit trenches. The next transit camp was twelve miles away at Bondi. By this time, late 1944, most of us hardly had any footwear and what clothing we possessed was used for patching and repatching the tatty scraps of material which acted as the shirt and shorts we used each day. The routing during the initial carrying of sacks was very dangerous as we had to watch where we walked when crossing small rivers and be especially wary of lurking predators camouflaged in the dense vegetation. Our main aim was survival, and on this particular working party we had, without doubt, the means for this at least as long as the job lasted. Before setting out on the eight mile trek, it was agreed the leader would set the pace somewhat quicker than average, so that the convoy became longer as the slower ones in the party dragged their heels. The idea was to stretch the convoy so that the guard at the rear of the convoy was unable to see the leading guard – simple but effective. It was not unusual to find that amongst the live animals being transported, a pig would be dead by the time we reached camp. As the Japanese would never touch animals found dead during transit they would offer it to the prisoners. With pig on our evening menu it made the unpolished rice taste as good as any served in a top class restaurant in London! It never really occurred to the Japanese what was happening, which was just as well, for we heard of many similar tales where prisoners were caught and they were never given the chance to try that ploy again.

Climbing the pathway up the steep hill towards Chilly Valley, each of us laden with sack loads of food, we would take a brief rest against a tree. Here, a Scot reached in his sack and handed me some brown sugar – the first sugar I had tasted since our capture. Another treat came when on our first day of travel near Chilly Valley; we climbed a steep hill and descending the other side, gazed to our amazement at what seemed to be a crystal-like bowl only four feet across – it was a spa. It was so still, so clear. We all gathered round with the same thought going through our minds – is it safe to drink? Our MO made the remark, 'Be it on your own heads'.

Apprehensively, each of us filled our mugs and drank the spring water – it was sparkling and pure with a hint of sweetness: it was the last of such water till our release. Today, it still provides me with an excellent illustration of the Water of Life. A month later, we had to pass that way once again and you can imagine our disappointment when we saw it had been trodden in by animals or maybe Japanese troops: it was now a mud hole.

When we were given a rest day it gave us a chance to wash and clean our dirty laundry, which only consisted of a bit of sacking and a threadbare blanket in need of de-lousing. Blood sucking white lice were always inside the lining or seams of what was left of our shorts and shirts and these caused us the most concern. Bed bugs were other unwelcome 'guests', making themselves at home in our blankets! I remember one frightening night when I was wakened by slimy wet feet scurrying across my face – it was a rat. I gave out such a loud shout the others sat bolt upright thinking it was another air raid!

Another item for de-lousing was one of my most treasured possessions – a small but firm pillow. Wherever we were commanded to sleep, whether on uneven cold soil, concrete or bamboo slats, if I had my pillow I always found I could sleep. During our weekly rest days, if all the work allocated was finished, we then had time to enjoy each other's company. One man, who had made his own chess set, would get a game going, another would try to provide some entertainment and, as we had no padre, being so small a party, one of the keener lads volunteered to lead an informal service. In places like this there was no talk of denomination. We soon began to realise those etched words on our ID tags were meaningless – we were all in the same predicament. As I think back over the years, I do recall meeting with some of the men who apparently experienced the Hand of God intervening in their lives during those testing times. It was different to my way of thinking; a man should keep those thoughts to himself rather than face ridicule from others in the camp. Even as I continued to read my little book, it was hard at times to avoid the heavier smokers in the camp trying to twist my arm to trade with them a few sheets of the very fine paper from my book. Apparently, it was ideal for their 'roll-ups', smoking a variety of leaves such as dried tea and banana leaves. Smoking these leaves may have been hazardous to health but they all survived!

In addition to the monkey, lizards, snakes and other reptiles, we were captivated by the numerous exotic butterflies and moths which would have been a lepidopterist's delight. There were also flying lizards and it was fascinating to study the chameleon's colour change as we chased them from differing parts of the colourful terrain. If only we had had a camera loaded with colour film – the scenes at dawn and sunset were unforgettable, the sky was flame red one minute, and the next a deep purple, then just as suddenly it would be pitch black.

Thoughts of home often flashed through our minds as we gazed to the heavens, although one very memorable day brought thoughts of London foremost in my mind. We were resting by a brook on our way towards Bondi, now only five miles away, when another working party approached from the south. We shared each others news. Although the men were from our Division we did not recognise any of them, but the group leader brought a much welcome reminder of home. He produced a stack of letters from England which had been in his possession for some weeks wondering if we knew any of the addressees. The names on the envelopes were shouted out – and most were for our party! Our rest period lasted quite a time as we read and re-read those most welcome letters. A letter can always bring news of disaster, hope, joy or sadness and we saw this reflected on the mens' faces many times over as they read their mail: someone killed in the bombing blitz over London, domestic problems, a failed marriage caused by the husband being trapped in a POW camp such as ours for nearly three years. Most of the letters I received had been writen over a period of six months and had all arrived together. Several were censored but this never bothered me as I was only glad to know my mother was well. I managed on one or two occasions to mention, in the limit of twenty five words, the name of a relation or friend who had written to me from England so as to indicate that I had received their letters. When I eventually returned I found out my plan had worked and they knew I was receiving mail – even if it was months late! To a number of young married men, or those with children, it was the end of the world if they never received a letter, often because the mail was thrown aside by the Japanese en route from India to Burma.

The taste of wholesome food, the regular supply of mail and all the good things in life have been doubly appreciated since our return.

Another year arrived – 1945, and still we were in captivity, without hope, other than the occasional vapour trail emblazoned across the sky from a Flying Fortress on its way to the South China Sea. The guards in this camp were quite reasonable, unlike the brutal individuals on the 'speedo' regime of the railway. Nicknames such as 'Doctor Death', 'The Kanyu Kid' and 'The Undertaker' were given to those notorious commandants, many of whom will never be forgotten.

Sitting in the camp area one evening, several of us were joined by a guard who conversed in excellent English and was as keen to return home as we were: he had a market garden where he developed a fine stock of chrysanthemums on the northern island of Hokkaido, and was often fearful of the news he was receiving concerning the war. Whilst most of the ordinary Japanese had no real knowledge of the progress towards victory from the Allied point of view, this one seemed to be conscious of the current situation. We were aware that the Allies were sweeping on to victory everywhere and now the focus was turning to South East Asian and Pacific sorties. Rangoon was under heavy attack and many of the islands in the Pacific were back in Allied hands. Sitting round the camp fire that evening, our guard was even hoping we might come to see him one day after it was all over. Our looks of amazement were sufficient for him to know that his offer was far from appreciated! After all these years, I often wonder if he ever did make it back to his family and small holding.

For the next few weeks the original road party was now back at the busy little transit camp opposite the Wampo sidings and just across the river. Whilst being a hive of activity, we were still well and truly hidden under the natural camouflage of the tall tamarind and bamboo trees which swept down to the edge of the swift flowing river and except for the sloping roadway to the jetty, it was well concealed – or so we thought. But all of a sudden one day several of us were flat on our faces in the dust at the jetty's edge. The reason being that, unknown to us as we worked in that morning sunlight, a Mosquito spotter plane had glided down over the mountain pass, through the valley and into the Wampo area, presumably reached the lowest safe altitude, and then opened the throttle for a quick ascent to its 30,000 feet normal altitude. As we took stock of the situation we were more than thankful we had not been machine-gunned. However, we remembered the similar experience back near Kanchanaburie and wondered whether this was a sign of things to come, the prelude for greater activity. Naturally, as we discussed this in the camp, we realised that some time we would be faced with the opportunity to escape, either by being in the centre of another fierce attack, or by some oversight on the part of the Japanese. We had not forgotten however that the Japanese could eliminate all of us if they so wished should the Allies approach our area. It was not a very encouraging thought but it was one we would have to face when the time came. Several of us with a warped sense of humour could not forget the initial reaction and the sight that presented itself as the aircraft had passed us: I'm sure our feet thought they were on a skating rink and we were going nowhere fast.

Our immediate task involved the transportation of supplies from the Station bank and across the river to the carefully secluded jetty to be loaded onto vehicles and then whisked away along the winding road towards Tavoy. The work was boring but bearable, for the guards were still maintaining a low profile in our camp.

It was a glorious day as we sat, midstream, on the ferry, which consisted of bamboo and teak planks lashed across two large barges, transporting goods to the other side. The ferry was laden with numerous vehicles and supplies. The deep river was, as usual, at its best, although we never sampled its coolness owing to the cholera warning and the small alligators and river snakes that frequented the area.

Then the tranquillity of our ferry voyage was disturbed once again as we heard the roar of a heavy bomber. It had been flying along the course of the river, rounded the mountain three miles away, and was now banking just above the trees in a curve towards us. Again, I have never seen a ferry move so fast to the jetty, with most of us lending assistance by leaping into the river with ropes in an attempt to haul the barges with us. As the plane roared past, probably only a few hundred feet above us, we saw clearly that it was a Flying Fortress with the Allied star markings on the fuselage. We even managed to pick out the rear gunners with side doors open revealing a large grille casing. It was dangerously yet thrillingly close, and yet no shots were fired from the plane although they could have blown us right out of the river. Was this another of those occasions when I was being reminded that the Lord had His hand very close to me and others also? This solitary plane alerted us to keep our eyes open for the rest of the day, in case the next visitor was not so friendly. We were dressed in what is commonly called 'G-strings', the same as the Japanese when out working, so it would be impossible to distinguish between us and the Japanese should we be attacked. Needless to say, the Japanese had no interest in the Geneva Convention and looked upon prisoners as a disgrace to their nation. Whether the American or Royal Air Forces based in the South East Asian theatre of war normally gave us much thought, they certainly did within the next few minutes! Another plane followed the same flight path as the previous one but this one had more fire power. Cannon fire came from both sides and the rear of the plane, any bombs presumably having been dropped on targets further up the river. For at least thirty minutes this plane put us through the mill as we sheltered behind tree trunks near the camp.

Since the first raid a year before in Hnong Pladuk, the planes had visited us in the afternoon. Now the bombers were in our area by early morning, this indicated that our Forces must be closing and getting nearer to our locations, perhaps out of Burma into Thailand. The only encouraging, if almost comical, raid we received at this time was a leaflet drop across the many areas where camps were sited. These colourful leaflets printed in English informed us to 'Look up, but keep your heads down!' and gave us news snatches from the bulletins providing us with a vague hope.

Locomotives were always mobile at night, and we lay on our bamboo beds listening to the chilling and eerie sound of the sirens echoing through the mountain valleys, across the river near the Wampo sidings. We now expected greater intensity from the Allied Forces. The war was now escalating after a relatively quiet two years in Malaya, Java and Sumatra. A heavy raid occurred several days later and was concentrated on the Wampo trestle bridge. Most of us sat on the edge of a dugout getting a ringside view of the attack. Several planes circled about four thousand feet above the cliff side, aiming for the bridge, but it seemed to take them an hour to destroy it. Following this, although we were at least three miles away, we made a speedy withdrawal into our dugouts, as the planes split formation and concentrated on bombing the Wampo sidings, our camp and other trains in the sidings. Fortunately, none of the lads were injured in the lengthy raid that followed. Several craters were made by bombs along the Wampo line: their size comparable to a double-decker bus. There were times when many of us wondered whether to wave to the aircraft, for in their low level approaches across our well hidden camp, we could easily make out the crew. But one wave could well have been our last movement, so we just sat tight and waited for the raid to end.

A tremendous forest fire developed one day which resulted in many square miles of the jungle being completely gutted. This caused us, if not the Japanese, great concern for our safety as the entire road, punctuated by small supply dumps, was now exposed and made an easy target from the air. As we extinguished the fires around our camp we realised the camp now stood out clearly. From our Wampo camp right up the road for some twenty miles, into Chilly Valley and onto Bondi – the entire stretch was stripped of its natural camouflage. We speculated on whether the devastation had been caused by a type of incendiary device or whether it was just another forest fire. Unless I ever meet someone who was on operations in the strategic Air Forces of South East Asia, I shall never know. Again, how slow one is to recognise the continual hand of the Lord in all these situations.

Some weeks later we were on the move once again and were thankful to pull out although not before we had been detailed to rebuild the bombed bridge at Wampo.

Moving out, thankfully by night, we travelled south, steaming out of Wampo. I need hardly say how fearful we felt as our train rolled across the bridge: we had been repairing it but we were by no means skilled engineers and we speculated whether or not we would make it to the other side! After listening to the ominous creaks of the bridge for about five minutes we breathed a sigh of relief as we crossed, incident free, and then moved on to our next destination.

7: God Keeps His Promise

The night was uneventful as we journeyed on our way south east, once again over the Kwai Bridge which was still intact, although it had been damaged several times in the previous months. Some miles south of Kanchanaburie we came to a halt, where we were ordered off and marched across open fields to a fairly large camp. Again we hurriedly looked around for long lost friends but alas mine were nowhere to be seen.

A week later we found we were on a further detail for a journey much longer than on previous occasions. The long train departed, this time during the day, and we all knew we would stand little chance if the Air Forces decided to survey the line east of Ban Pong. Our train joined the main junction and travelled east passing Hnong Pladuk, which now appeared to us as a kind of ghost town. We began to relive the tragic experience of a year previously when so many were killed that night in 1944. The train chugged on and, about an hour later, passed one of the most spectacular pagodas we had seen, its huge base coloured emerald green. Eventually, we pulled into a small siding on the outskirts of Bangkok. Then, with no time to see the great city of the east, we were taken down to board large barges anchored at the banks of a wide river, the barges being drawn by streamline motorboats and each brightly decorated in the Thai national colours. The river trip along the winding curves lasted an hour before we were ushered from the barges alongside the 'go-downs' or docks onto a freight train. By then we were on the east side of the city, and this could only indicate that we were heading towards Cheingmai, or perhaps Ubon towards the Indo-China border. Whichever it was, we now felt we were being moved as far away from the war zone as possible, giving us little hope of imminent release. No sooner were we locked in the wooden trucks that we heard the city air raid sirens, followed by the familiar sound of our bombers as they flew freely around Bangkok. We were not exactly in the most favourable position – high up on the dock side in a train that could easily have contained Japanese supplies! But here we were, and again, I'm sure the hand of God was very much upon us. Some time after the all-clear, the Japanese and Thai workers returned and the train moved off and rumbled over small bridges and through open plains with palm and other fruit trees scattered along the route.

Many hours later we were told to get out and we realised we had not travelled as far as Indo-China, nor were we north of Bangkok heading for Cheingmai but were out in the country about one hundred and fifty miles north east of Bangkok. There was one clue, however: we were now only a short distance from the beginning of a long range of high hills sloping away to the north, punctuated with several steep rocks towering hundreds of feet above the remainder of the hills. We thought we must be near the small town of Saraburie and rumour had it that we were in the area of a place called Pratchai. Wherever we were, we noticed we had a contingent of Japanese artillery almost within our camp, which did little to comfort us. As usual, there was always a reason for a move and it was not for our benefit! Working parties were soon required to commence excavating large areas at the foot of the hills, presumably to use as shelters at a later date. The routine of the days went by the same as any other: there was certainly no noise of bombers.

As in most camps, the hospital wards were little different from huts, although they varied in the little extra comfort provided in the way of additional sacking or blankets. The MOs were kept very busy, especially with the outbreak of blackwater fever added to the increasing number of cases of malaria and dysentery – it seemed an endless task. When would the end really come?

It was now the middle of 1945 – and once again I had developed a fever with a high temperature meaning the next few days would be spent in the hospital: it was the fifth time I had contracted malaria. However, as in any time of trouble, there is always a brighter side, particularly when there are many praying for you so many miles away. I was thankful I was still managing to survive, even with a tropical ulcer on one leg, bacillary dysentery, and at one time septic scabies. Could it have been because of the wholesome diets which my family had provided, even through the depression, and that I had never had the urge to smoke or drink at anytime in my life? Had all this given me the basics for good stamina for all these years or was it that, somehow, a spiritual figure was watching over me? I often wonder, even to this day, how during those three weeks of fierce fighting in Singapore, I, with several others in the Royal Corps of Signals, was never faced with the awful situation of having to kill to survive.

It was in this camp, a few days following my malarial attack and trying to find something to occupy myself, that I decided to take another look at my book: there was not anyone around on this morning to notice. But somehow the book accidentally slipped from my hand and fell open across my bed space. Retrieving it, still open, my eyes seemed to be transfixed by three lines of the open page. It

almost appeared as though the rest of the open pages had
been blotted out. The words stood out appearing to be
bolder than the rest of the print. How strange but how
remarkable, here was my companion book, which had
survived with me the three and a quarter years. The words
I read, and read again were '. . . when the heaven was
shut up three years and six months, when great famine was
throughout all the land . . .' That may not seem to mean
very much initially, but to a prisoner, under the heel of the
Japanese for over three years, surviving the most gruelling
experiences, then these words were full of hope. I looked
again, and re-read it. Could it be saying that we would be
free of the camps within the three and a half years? Was
God in some way giving me a promise? After all, had He
not in some amazing way delivered me during that air raid
when I cried to Him a year previously? I began to tell
several of my mates and you can imagine the reaction.
'God does not do things like that', 'That's all right for the
Sunday School class or those who are "religious", but for
soldiers it's different!'

My father had carried this New Testament during his
service with the Royal Scots Greys all those years ago and I
was sure it was no accident that I carried the same book
and was riveted to those three lines found in Luke 4.25.

The amazing point on this direct word from the Holy
Scriptures was that it was foretelling our day of freedom.
That was what I was thinking, but would it happen? Two
months to elapse, not very long to find out. The days went
by into weeks, then came August, and finally the day of
the 16th, 1945 dawned.

It was a day with a difference, but not the way my
simple mind was working. The Japanese urgently called
for several hundred prisoners to parade with their kit,
hardly giving them time to collect their thoughts. They

were off to construct a large emergency airstrip many miles beyond the mountain range. This rather sudden decision on that morning tested my new found faith and yet in a certain, unavoidable sense, it seemed that something big was about to happen. Noon came and not much to report; the same unpolished rice with a small splattering of green vegetable stew, an occasional shout and scream between a guard and an unfortunate prisoner who happened to be in the wrong place at the wrong time! The afternoon began to show signs of slipping towards evening when suddenly, several vehicles arrived at the camp gates – it was the unexpected return of the working party which had left in the morning. They were back, so was my excitement, but why? An hour later we heard, for the first time in three and a half years, the orderly calling everyone on parade, with his trumpet to lips in true British style! Great excitement swelled up within us as we rushed to our normal parade positions. The leading NCO made the announcement, 'The war has ended . . .' 'It's finished! We've made it!!' Shouts of celebration filled the air throughout the whole camp. We leapt for joy. We wept. It seemed as if we would not stop. The Japanese in the adjacent camp were resting. What was going to happen? The Union Jack was already being hoisted in place of the Rising Sun, but after a discussion with the Japanese Commandant, our NCO decided to play it cool until our Allied Forces arrived, so our flag was put to one side for a while. Though euphoric, the next few days were potentially dangerous for us. No massive army came for us, in fact one paratrooper walked in and a solitary bomber flew over giving us a victory roll as it passed, dropping a few luxuries for us. We were conscious of the large array of Japanese military equipment all around us. Patience was essential and eventually officials arrived with orders for our withdrawal from Pratchai. It had taken a few days for the Japanese authorities to provide details to the SEAC Commands of where all the prisoners would be found in Thailand: some in large camps near Bangkok, Kanchanaburie, others in jungle areas where they could easily have been missed.

Inoculations against the dreaded smallpox and other fevers were given to us, and within a week, that September, we prepared for what was going to be the best journey of our lives. We mounted the vehicles, with more comfort and space for each of us and even though it was an open truck it was a marvellous feeling. Some hours after we left camp, we were informed that we could have been in serious trouble had any of the lads decided to take the law into their own hands and have a go at settling the score. But one could never settle this score – after all that the Japanese had done to the prisoners. There were no Allied troops anywhere near and we were advised that even the ordinary Japanese soldier had no idea the war was over. Having lost, their propaganda machine had provided them with other ideas. And so, once again, we were protected in some way by an unseen Hand.

The full extent of how we came to be released so suddenly never fully dawned on us until we were out of Thailand. An atomic bomb had been dropped on Nagasaki and then on Hiroshima and their terrifying results are still in evidence today.

During the long bumpy trip with a Japanese driver and British trooper up front in our lorry, the journey was a joy-ride for us all. It was hard to grasp the reality of the situation – we were actually free! I remember many of the tough lads shedding a tear, perhaps for the first time. From a personal point of view, the amazing message from my Testament began to materialise in a way far greater as each minute ticked by. Here was this word of God telling me months before of coming freedom and we were freed exactly three and a half years after being made prisoners. It was not the previous day or the day after – it was that very day. There was no padre in this camp, and as far as I was concerned probably no so-called Christians either. It was the Holy Spirit which revealed this day of freedom, and ever since that day I have realised that there is only one Person you can really trust and lean upon, no matter how tough the going gets. Recalling the many near misses in my life, the bombing raid, and the deliverance when I cried to the Lord, and the day of freedom from His word, I began to wonder: this is something different to what I had been used to in the church I attended each week in Walthamstow. How then, can one really get in contact with this God who, during the last three and a half years, had shown so many times that His hand was over me and directing my life? My little book seemed to hold the key. Did it, I wondered?

8: Liberty with Abundant Life

Many hours elapsed before we eventually exchanged our somewhat bumpy journey on unmade roads for a much smoother ride on a concrete surface. Entering the perimeter road, we reached Bangkok airport located several miles from the city centre; once again we had missed the opportunity of even catching a glimpse of the city itself.

The convoy of lorries drew in close to a neat line-up of air transport carriers, many of which were the highly respected DC-3, or Dakota as it is more commonly known. The majority of us had never experienced a flight before and any worries concerning this aspect of our freedom would be left till we were in the air. Each aircraft had space for twenty five passengers and the planes had been hastily adapted for our comfort. It was with great relief to be receiving the more favourable hospitality from the RAF than previously experienced with the bombing raids. Delighted to be sitting comfortably in this new form of transport, it was not long before the engines burst into life, awaiting flight clearance and instructions from the control tower recently acquired from the Japanese. Within minutes we were taxiing to the far end of the concrete runway approach, steadily turning and facing west into a slight breeze. There was, however, a growing concern amongst us as the Dakota gathered speed to take-off – with all their pre-flight checks they had forgotten to close the door! It was only when the pilot reassured us that these planes were used for parachuting troops and doors were never fitted that we calmed down; nevertheless several of us inched our way further up the plane, just in case of any unforseen incidents! By now we were cruising at around six thousand feet and with clear skies we were treated to magnificent views of the jungle. It did not take long for us to identify the River Kwai and the railroad of death winding together through the dark green vegetation. The flight took two hours and was extremely pleasant and interesting, especially as the flight crew allowed each of us to browse over the flight deck. As we left Thailand far below, we saw to our portside the wide expanse of deep blue water which we were informed was the Sea of Martaban, whilst looking towards the starboard we saw in sharp contrast, a mountain range sloping into jungle surroundings which reached as far as the horizon and reminded us of the horrors we had experienced during the previous three years – memories that would linger for the rest of our lives.

Whilst the journey was an experience of a lifetime, I was feeling far from well and the reason was not due to any form of air travel. My right arm was causing considerable pain: it had been aching during the previous few days and the trouble centred on the vaccine scratches given when the mass medical screening against smallpox had been administered a week previously. The rather dirty plaster was peeling off my arm, the size of which was gradually increasing, as was my temperature. We watched with wonderment, the many irregularly shaped white fluffy clouds slipping by the windows and by the open door, the sun was glinting far in the distance on the large golden tower of Swedagon Pagoda and we knew this must be our destination. We were slowly losing height and directly ahead was the Burmese capital – Rangoon. Our plane circled, giving all of us our first experience of landing preparations. We had regained a bit of our courageous spirit, for many now stood by the open doorway holding firmly to the edge and viewing the city.

All military transport was landing at the emergency metal runways of Mingladon. The landing was perfect and many army vehicles awaited our arrival, backing up to each aircraft once the engines stopped. Most of the vehicles displayed the familiar sign of the Red Cross and so the next phase of our journey home was under way.

Special emergency field unit hospitals had been established, some only in operation for days prior to our arrival, following the rapid ceasefire throughout South East Asia.

The British General Hospital was situated close to the Victoria Lake in the grounds of Rangoon University. Here our documentation was quickly and efficiently carried out for everyone, except that, following a quick medical screening, I found myself being channelled in the opposite direction from most of my colleagues. Evidently my swollen arm had caused this setback, although there was so much to occupy my mind I quickly forgot my infected arm. The military personnel were in smart army green uniforms and suits with neat bush hats, similar to those worn by the Australian soldiers when we first saw them on entering Singapore.

For the first time in nearly four years we saw our first white ladies – the Nursing Officers of the Queen Alexandra's Imperial Military Nursing Services. Once we were in the environment of the hospital confines the nurses were everywhere. That first night is another that will never be forgotten as we climbed between the spotless white sheets and laid our heads on most comfortable and soft pillows. The following morning we were kitted out

71

with modern tropical clothes, the first we had worn in four years. On entering Rangoon the only clothes I had were a pair of well worn blue shorts and my only possession, my New Testament – that was all! All footwear, shirts and hats had worn out several years previously. After realising many of my friends were going straight to a large transit camp far outside Rangoon ready for their long voyage home, I was beginning to get rather apprehensive – after all, three and a half years in a Japanese prisoner of war camp, and now to be placed in a Military Hospital! For how long, I wondered?

The hospital had its regular routines, as I was to understand from that first day. The morning medical inspection, followed by treatment; in my case it was administered by an exceedingly attractive dark haired Nursing Officer. Her course of treatment made an immediate impression on me! Even before I was able to yell, she had stripped off my plaster, thickly coated with mucus, exposing a badly inflamed area on the upper section of my right arm. The septic ulcer was duly given the best treatment and I soon established that this Nursing Sister was a Scot; my ancestors on my father's side had resided in the village of Auchtermuchty and I lost no time in telling her this.

In her bright white tropics uniform, she certainly provided a breath of the sweetest air to me. As she firmly fixed the new plaster with precision, as only nurses can, we exchanged a few brief comments on the locations and positions we had visited during the war period. I continued to fuel the conversation discussing the main topics of the day. We had never heard of such things as the V1 and V2 rockets, the appalling massacres within the gas chambers in Nazi held territory, or the unbelievably horrific bombs which had been dropped on Hiroshima and Nagasaki – and yet had secured the release for each of us in the camps of South East Asia. However, one item happened to catch the keen eyes of this Scots nurse – my New Testament.

She curiously picked it up and began opening it with interest. It was not long before we were deeply engrossed in conversation on the strange and unique events I had been experiencing, although I rather shyly admitted that I had cried to the Lord during the air raid. I eagerly mentioned, however, the amazing way in which I had been given what looked like a prophecy from my book; how that we would be free men within the three and a half years – and to be actually free before that day ended! Wondering how long we were going to continue in this vein, I was astonished to hear from her lips, as she turned several pages that she seemed to know her way round almost every chapter of my book. She very confidently showed me from the very book which I had carried over five years, how 'God so loved the World, that He gave His only begotten Son, that whosoever believeth in Him should not perish, but have everlasting life', and it was not long before she followed this bombshell with another – that I, like everyone else, 'had sinned and come short of the glory of God'. The conversation was beginning to get a bit personal: and uncomfortable too, and yet everything the Nursing Officer said, I had to admit, was coming to me with authority – not military authority but with conviction.

I had been reading this one book for the past three and a half years – and within a few moments she introduced me to its author, Jesus Christ! It makes all the difference in the world when you come to really *know* the author of *this* book! Only a few weeks previously, following the day of freedom, I had been wondering how to get in touch with a

God who delivers in an air raid, who gives a promise in His book, and keeps it to the very day. Now in a hospital in Rangoon, the Lord was giving the answers so soon, which showed me that if we are ever sincerely seeking or thirsting for the Lord, His Holy Spirit will never leave us without bringing us into the truth through His word and by His witnesses. This first somewhat shattering and yet amazing discussion with the nurse, was not to be the last, not by a long way – it was only the beginning. This trim attractive nurse, dressed in white cap and uniform for daytime duty and equally smart tunic, slacks and headband for night duty, shared a little of her own Christian experience back in the United Kingdom. It was whilst she had attended at an early age, a Faith Mission convention in her home town in Fife, that she became a Christian. She informed me that being a Christian was a considerable help in one's daily life wherever one worked and I really knew she meant what she said. I spent nearly three weeks in hospital, eagerly looking forward to the daily discussions which would occur during any off-duty period. We continued to meet and discuss a variety of interesting topics but in nearly every conversation we returned to the all important subject – the Christian way of life. Much of what I was hearing was certainly new to me, and was not exactly the Christianity I had been familiar with before the war. However, the more we talked, the more I was beginning to see things differently and much more clearly.

A very remarkable thing happened to me whilst in Rangoon, although it was not until many years later that I was to fully experience the evidence of what happened to me in the hospital on that day. Up until the day before I had received my medical treatment from the Nursing Officer, I, like all the other ex-prisoners, vehemently hated and detested the Japanese and their very name, for the ill treatment they had meted out to us. However, the moment I surrendered my life to Jesus, as the Nursing Officer introduced me to my Saviour, it was as if all thought of hatred and bitterness had gone. How could this be?

The so-called three weeks 'training course' in discipleship I was receiving from the nurse brought about a delightful mixture of friendship and fellowship, eventually developing into a deeper interest in each other. However, the day for departure from Rangoon dawned and having to say farewell with such an understanding and helpful nurse as this one was like departing from someone I had known most of my life. How strange and unexpected that this had all come about. She had been an instrument in starting to unlock the many treasures contained in my father's book; she had brought so much to me and here I was, just about to leave: would I ever see her again? I was returning to England a different person. I knew something had happened but what was it? It was all so new to me but, without a doubt, whatever it was, it was real.

The journey home was lengthy but gave most of us a chance to recuperate, calling through Colombo, Suez, the Red Sea and on into the Mediterranean. Finding anyone I could relate to on the journey proved impossible, so I contented myself with the thoughts of the first three glorious weeks in Rangoon. My mind continued to retrace its steps to Rangoon and the nurse. I recalled she had mentioned she attended a Baptist Church. I wondered what type of a church that could possibly be. Being an Anglican this was the only denomination I had any knowledge of, except of course, for my young days when I had attended a Methodist Church Sunday School. The mention of these other denominations somewhat puzzled me, although they never bothered me in any way before the war. Such terminology as 'Missions', 'Evangelistic Crusades', 'Tent Campaigns', were a bit unusual to my way of thinking. Somehow everything she had said during our time together in Rangoon seemed to be very right. Could it be, I wondered, that in some unique way I had come through to what was termed a 'conversion' experience? I was very glad that I still had my New Testament for the journey home, for, no doubt, it was becoming a living word to me. Turning over in my mind the events of the previous four years, I can never thank the Lord enough for bringing me out of the horrific jungle camps of Thailand and for helping me regain my health and strength, again very remarkable when I consider the many thousands who died for their country. I thought of the crosses that marked their place of death and the memory of them all, particularly my closest friends. And, as I thought of these crosses, I seemed to become aware of one large cross covering all the small crosses, the cross on which Jesus Christ had died for our sin, our sickness, our fears and apprehensions – He had taken it all on that cross at Calvary, for each of us. And all He asks of us today is that we take Him at His word and enter into all that He accomplished on that cross – knowing that our redemption is forever settled in Him.

We were making good time through the Mediterranean, around Gibraltar and into the Bay of Biscay, which was kind to us considering its normal turbulence. A few days later we were entering the Channel of St George, Anglesey and finally the port of Liverpool.

It was a dull November day as we disembarked after the three week journey and the year of 1945 was rapidly coming to a close: so much had happened during that momentous year. The dockside welcome was tremendous where the efficiency of the RTO was in keeping with the occasion. Display signs provided information to each of us to ensure a quick exit by train to all parts of the country. Within an hour the London bound train departed from Liverpool and we were soon in the English countryside – reviving memories of bygone days. It takes situations such as we had encountered to make us appreciate everything, whether our life, our home, our food and even to know that we could now, at the turn of a tap, drink ice-cool water without the effort of boiling it first. I even recall one or two very bad nightmares in Thailand, when I, and others, dreamed we were about to gorge ourselves with chocolate bars or the best of British food – they were nightmares, for we woke just prior to getting even a taste!

At Euston Station the fleet of ambulances was armed with keen and efficient Red Cross personnel, arranging for us to be transported with the least amount of trouble to our various homes. With our new kit, issued as we left the boat, we climbed into an ambulance. There were five others with me, all bound for the north east area around London. It was good to be back in England after so long out of touch with everything. The ambulance soon began to deliver the lads; Shoreditch, then Hackney, Leyton-stone and finally Walthamstow. As I made a quick exit from the vehicle, giving a well appreciated thank you to the lady driver, I surveyed home. It was gone six in the evening and all was in darkness. Just as I was about to knock on the door lights blazed, music began all around, and neighbours opened their doors to join with my mother in welcoming me home. Homecomings like this became frequent events immediately the war ended. Words cannot express all you want to say in a situation like this, when one has endured separation, without news, for so many years.

I settled down very quickly. The days soon slipped by

into December and I was continually pondering on the amazing weeks I had spent in Rangoon, wondering how my Nursing Officer was progressing and trying to relive some of the words of wisdom she had given to me from the Scriptures. The sharing of my experiences from the New Testament came quickly, first with my mother and then with a number of relatives. Whilst my mother appreciated much of what I had found from the Scriptures, it received a cool reception from others.

I was anxious to rebuild the career that I had set out upon prior to the outbreak of war. This meant searching the Fleet Street area for an advertising agency until eventually I secured a position within a well-established company.

9: A Partnership for all Time

January 10th in the new year of 1946 was another of those great days of my life. It started early for me as I eagerly waited on a crowded platform in King's Cross Station to meet the overnight express from Scotland. I was due to meet a very important passenger. I waited anxiously at the barrier, hoping my visitor had not missed the train. Suddenly, as the crowds pushed past either side of the barrier, a space appeared, and there she was – a most attractive young woman, carrying a suitcase and still in uniform. Even at this early hour her blue eyes sparkled and she gave me a melting smile. My first words were not what she expected. . . .'How would you like to get married today?' and I continued before she had time to say otherwise . . . 'at three o'clock this afternoon'. That afternoon, the Nursing Officer from the Rangoon Military Nursing Hospital became my wife! It was just under four months since our first meeting in Rangoon, where I received my first promise from the Lord, followed by another equally important direction from the New Testament in the hospital a few days after our first meeting. We had prayed and sought the Lord together about our future and we both found for ourselves the verse which gave us our direction; 'He that hath the Bride is the Bridegroom . . .' (John 3.29). After thirty eight happy years both of us can say truly that we have never regretted the day we came to that vital decision to start life together. It gets better each year! All through our lives together we can indeed say we have repeatedly proved the Lord through His word and have found it to be a word that never fails or passes away. 'The Word of God is quick and powerful and sharper than any two edged sword,' perhaps I might even add – any two edged Japanese sword!

As my first place of employment continued for two years we set up home in the London suburb of Chingford. Agnes, my wife, was keen to find a local church, a church which would help to encourage us both in the basics of the Bible-based teaching so necessary for Christian living. Within a few streets of our home we found one: it was a Congregational church! I was certainly increasing my education as far as other denominations were concerned. My wife was a good judge when it came to the type of church with which we should identify ourselves. It was soon obvious she did have that discernment; the church consisted of a combination of missionary vision and an evangelistic outreach mixed with pastoral care for all the members and visitors. These basic qualities were confirmed in the years ahead for us all as the expanding work under the anointing of the Holy Spirit brought a deeper ministry in the word of God. To supplement this steady work of the Lord in our midst came the news of a decision by the Evangelical Alliance to invite an American Evangelist, Dr. Billy Graham, to come to London to lead a crusade. It was 1954 and I made another of those important and worthwhile steps in my Christian experience as interest and momentum gathered during the months preceding the great event. There was a growing sense of unity as many churches of most denominations came together to offer their services and to assist in the many avenues available for the crusade. Specialised counsellor training courses, lasting several weeks, were a great encouragement to us all. These courses, attended by several hundred people in each venue, were held in and around London. The lasting benefits derived from the classes have confirmed the need for good systematic Bible instruction for every Christian. For nearly three long months, the Greater London Crusade, held in Harringay Stadium, saw many from our local church engaged in stewardship, counselling, advising and choir activities. Most evenings during the entire period of the crusade there would be a steady flow of people coming from all directions to converge on Manor House. Trains on the Piccadilly Lines arrived with many of the workers supporting the crusade; as the doors opened, they would release a great flood of people destined for the stadium.

They came in thousands; professionals, show business personalities, sports personalities, business people, the ordinary working person and the media from many corners of the world – to report on this phenomenon. Every night, with the arena packed, many needy people in their hundreds responded. With very little persuasion at nine o'clock, Billy Graham would give the invitation, 'To come . . .' and the people came, every night for the whole duration of the event. It was remarkable to note the way in which the Lord so often brought the particular person alongside the counsellor who had been the way of the enquirer himself many years previously. During the thirty years since the crusade, I, for one, have met many who responded to that altar call in Harringay and are now involved in a fruitful ministry of some kind, confirming the lasting results of those many prayer intercessors during the early days of 1954. For the first time I experienced what was termed an 'All night of prayer'. Before the crusade I had never heard of such an experience and it was far from what I thought it was going to be – it had a pulsating power of great expectancy from ten in the evening till six the following morning.

During the crusade we decided to hold informal prayer meetings in our home each week and one morning a poster displayed on our window caught the eye of a passer-by. Answering the door we were met by a police officer! He showed interest and asked to join the prayer meetings as he was actively involved in the Christian Police Association. Opening the door to that policeman also opened the door to a great friendship and fellowship, still strong to this day. When the Lord introduces us to friends they turn out to be lasting companions as we soon discovered. Two other such lasting friendships came in a similar way. One Ernest Raisey, the former General Secretary of the Post Office Christian Association and, prior to his passing, a Minister of the Elmstead Lane Baptist Church. His wife, Margaret, now continues a great ministry of intercession and counselling for ladies. Since those days of the crusade, I, like others in the publicity profession have been approached by numerous enthusiastic Christians wanting to move quickly on the same approaches and procedures as were seen in the Greater London Crusade.

In those years as a publicity man and a Christian, I was beginning to learn that the Lord rarely wants us to copy another person, his ministry, or his work. I was beginning to recognise the Lord never seems to repeat patterns in His way of working out His purpose. I would suggest if any person, church, or committee, is considering launching into a publicity campaign for any work, no matter how large or small it may be, to wait upon the Lord for His leading and direction. The Lord will always give exacting directions, whether to launch out and spend considerable amounts of money in media advertising; or to gather a group together for prayer; or not hold the crusade, as it might not be the correct time for an outreach work as the important ministry might still be required within the church itself. In parts of Timor and Indonesia it was reported by several authentic missionaries and ministers that not one handbill was printed in many of the areas when the Holy Spirit directed and gathered thousands to meet at points during the revivals which swept through those countries not long ago. Numerous books have been published which confirm this wonderful work of grace. Whatever the Lord says in any work, particularly where public relations are concerned, then we should heed His word and leading. The results are so much more rewarding and far less frustrating. Following the London Crusade a noticeable desire was evident amongst the youth of the church for an ongoing work within their lives and this did not go unnoticed by the older members. As with other churches in the country, there was a steady build up in the numbers attending the weekly prayer and Bible classes as a spiritual awakening was beginning to stir amongst all Christians in practically all denominations. To us as a family we were more than thankful to be based in a good place of fellowship, especially as our two sons began to grow up. Much of our life was centred around the work and outreach of the church; many well known Bible teachers would share the regular Saturday night rallies where others from a great distance would join us. Visiting speakers from as far as Africa, Formosa, New Zealand, Papua, and Canada shared their testimonies. During the twenty six years of encouragement in the fellowship of this particular church, one did not have to consider in engaging for a 'weekend retreat' or 'convention' – the full activities of the normal healthy church was a convention in itself each week. The European Secretary of the WEC visited our church one weekend and gave us first-hand details of the work of the Lord throughout parts of Timor and the Dutch East Archipelago. These were years of valuable training for which we were truly thankful in the days that lay ahead in ministry, learning from many talented people.

Our two sons eventually left home, one to become engaged in work as an ophthalmic optician at a London eye hospital and the other deciding to enter the advertising profession.

Taking teams out from the church provided me with a greater experience in ministering at other churches and fellowships. Our team would consist of the keen youngsters from the fellowship who would be an encouragement, not only to themselves, but to the people they visited. Ministering in a few of the pulpits brought some smiles and interest as we noticed the discreet messages fixed within the pulpit so as to catch the eyes of the speakers; such notices ranged from 'Sirs, we would see Jesus' – which was a comforting reminder, to 'Make sure you finish the service by seven thirty prompt.' With the increased interest around the country in the growing renewal work, evangelistic campaigns, numerous churches being revived and some denominational churches which had been drifting into despair for so long – we soon became aware of the growing activities in the occult and other evil forces at work by Satan. Fortunately, as with this acceleration, so there was a similar growth in the lives of new Christians who really meant business for the Lord Jesus Christ as they studied the word of God and became involved in prayer intercession, to join with others in praise and worship. It was interesting to note that many of these young people who became Christians in a comparatively short time were being used in ministries whilst many of us older Christians of twenty years experience were being challenged – they were moving forward and we are thankful to the Lord for this great increase by the younger generation.

10: Working as a Christian in Advertising

I had just reached the top floor of the two-storey building, near the Street of Ink – Fleet Street. The reason for my visit was that a position in a new, up-and-coming advertising agency was vacant. Two directors listened intently to my application and, after leaving me in a small office for a brief period, returned and asked when I could start. I informed them that I was a Christian and would prefer not to handle advertising for alcohol or tobacco, or anything overtly sexual. They heard my somewhat hesitant testimony – and they agreed; I got the job. This particular acknowledgement in honouring the Lord confirmed to me later how He kept His promise – for during the next thirteen years never once did the agency chiefs ask me to handle advertising that I felt was unsavoury. Many times since, when engaged in publicity campaigns, I have been confronted with the problem client, who in his enthusiasm to obtain a better image, considers featuring the female figure amidst his engineering products. Every time the Lord would give me a word of wisdom and positively reveal how respect for the prestige of such a long established company would be undermined from his own customers and how few nuts and bolts would be sold because an undressed figure featured in the advertisement.

Being a Christian, on your own, in any business, is always a life of adventure and challenge. My first challenge came not many days after joining the new company. The financial director handed me a pad, pen and a selection of London telephone directories, pointed to my desk telephone and said, 'We need more business, now, so it's up to you!' I was stunned as these words rang in my ears. I had never sold a thing in my life – what kind of position had I got myself into this time? With some apprehension, mixed with a touch of panic, I could think of only one thing – prayer! As I thumbed through the directory I began to pray about the situation. My colleagues in the office were preoccupied with other work. As I silently called to the Lord, I was aware once again of the nearness of the Saviour who had delivered me on many previous occasions. Within seconds the name of a businessman flashed through my mind; some months previously I had attended a meeting at which I made contact with a friendly Scot. He was an advertising manager of several industrial publications. I dialled his number, waited, and was soon in conversation with him on the generalities of business. He invited me to his office the next day. I was glad to be out on what I would term as business research work and, following a welcome cup of coffee, steered my way towards asking where one could possibly obtain business in these days. Advertising managers of most publications are usually aware if their advertisers are satisfied with their agencies. My Scots friend seemed to appreciate my predicament and, picking up a current copy of his journal, proceeded to thumb through it. Very soon I found myself noting the names of companies who, at that time, were not using the services of advertising agents. Within an hour I was on my way with several names to contact. So far so good, but now followed the tricky bit – how to handle a direct contact?

Next day, back at the desk, I studied my list carefully

and eventually decided who to ring first, quickly rehearsing in my mind how to open the conversation. I dialled a number in the Paddington area and waited as the ringing continued for several seconds before there was a reply from what seemed to be an elderly person. Carefully choosing my words, I gave the reason for my call and somehow managed to capture his interest: an appointment was made for the following week. I made quick but silent acknowledgement to the Lord for this first call, mixed with a certain amount of relief. A week later I was off down the steps into Blackfriars Station, where I boarded a westbound tube for Paddington. I negotiated the heavy traffic and reached my destination. The approach to the building was uninviting. I entered dimly lit showrooms and as I climbed the stairs to the reception I could not help but notice a strong chemical odour which lingered in each room I entered. Finally, I was shown into a small office where the elderly gentleman was waiting. The office had a Victorian air and each piece of furniture was well stacked with out-of-date technical journals and box files. Here I was, facing what could be my first client and yet this seemed to be the last place one would expect to discuss advertising. Surprisingly however, I obtained the account and in the ensuing period found the answer to the strong odour I encountered in various parts of the building – my work was to market butane and propane gas.

The first account, which the Lord had opened to me for the company, resulted in us handling part of the actual chemical company some years later. I was beginning to learn that whether at home or in business, a testimony cannot always linger in the past but must be a daily experience.

After seven years things were going exceptionally well for the company and all the employees benefited. I really began to feel I was doing well and it is not a wise thing when you start as a Christian to think in this fashion – as I was soon to find out. For some reason, that year, the source of my supply of business rapidly diminished for no apparent reason and it was not long before I was aware of the situation – it was drying up for me! During one of the weekly production meetings I was reminded, in no uncertain terms, of the worsening position. My first reaction, as with most of us in this big commercial world of Fleet Street, was panic – something had to be done. It is often in a situation like this that the Lord has His way of proving us in line with His word. As I found out, the directors of the company had no qualms over my perform-ance during the previous years especially when targets were reached and increased each month. However, if the results are reversed then the true feelings begin to emerge, rapidly. How was I going to obtain business so quickly and to the amounts required to save my face and pride at a time like this? My first mistake came as I left the office shortly after six that evening knowing the managing director was going to haul me over the coals the next day.

Where could I get help? Then I knew where to go; I headed for Liverpool Street. I knew one of my business friends would still be working at his office near Finsbury Square. Many times in the past I had joined Ted and Jim for prayer – sometimes three times a day, before work, lunchtime and after office hours. They were very profit-able times but somehow, recently, I had not allocated much time for this essential period of intercession. As I sat in a comfortable chair opposite Ted he appeared to me to be much happier and more joyful than usual. He shared a little of his new found peace, as he called it, and how, through the word of the Lord, he had come to enter into many of God's promises as never before. He told me his prayer life had been revolutionised and his reading of the Scriptures was like reading a daily newspaper – the word was alive to him. He was also noticing a change in his own attitude to others – particularly other Christians. In place of differences, he was finding a new dimension of what could only be termed the compassion, love and under- standing of the Lord within his life. Being anxious not to show my immediate anxiety, I continued to listen patiently and knew that I had been missing something since I had stopped taking time with the Lord in joining with the others at their daily retreat. It was not long before Ted began to discern my reason for the unexpected visit; he could see through the curtain overshadowing my face – and I knew it! He listened to my sad tale, which was certainly not a testimony of victory, and when I eventually got round to my reason for being in his office, I was somewhat stunned by his answer and reaction! Ted, being the managing director of an electronic company had, within his power, the authority for engaging my services as an advertising agent if he desired. In my rather selfish way I naturally assumed he had the answer for my predica- ment. Ted always had a gentle and understanding approach to anyone he spoke with and was always a help to me. He suggested that we ought to pray and, descending to our knees, we did. My friend was in close contact with the Lord, and I felt the presence of the Saviour during the following half-hour. It was a time of praise, worship and adoration of the Lord's great goodness to us. As we closed in prayer I somewhat feebly added a few 'Amens'. Ted looked me right in the eye and informed me very sincerely that the Lord had told him not to give me any business! That was certainly a blow below the belt for me coming from my closest friend! Then he continued to remind me of my commitment to the Lord, pointing out that after all, this situation had first of all got me to my knees. He was right but I was not admitting it there. Finally, he reminded me of the Scriptures, 'In all things give thanks to Him, for this is the will of God concerning us,' and then the final parting shot before we sat back in our respective chairs, 'Why don't you say thank you for nothing. . .' I left his office somewhat dejected and feeling very sorry for myself. It was hardly the answer I was expecting when he had the ability to help me. Later that night, after my wife went to bed, I sat down, thinking about the events of the day and the time spent with Ted. I pondered over the words again and again, 'Why not say thank you for nothing. . .' I had thought earlier that day, that it was a strange thing to say to me, but now somehow it was not so strange, it was beginning to make sense. Now I was facing business difficulties and yet I was not carrying out the request from the Holy Scriptures – 'In all things to give thanks'. It was midnight, I had nothing to lose and I knew what the Scriptures had indicated on previous occasions when I had been reading 1 Thessalonians 5.18. It is easy to read but hard to believe and do it. There was no other way out, I had to come and surrender my pride, the whole situation and my failure to join regularly with others in prayer. And I found out later, I must not lean on my Christian friends instead of Jesus. I was quietly saying to the Lord, 'Thank you Lord for where I am tonight, I'm sorry for the way I have gone over the past months and thank you for nothing'. I found myself confessing to Jesus, I was really meaning what I prayed. I am so thankful I did.

The following day, for some reason, the much publicised production meeting was cancelled, providing me, I thought, with a little extra time to *worry* about the problem, but it was not to be. My telephone rang bringing me back to reality: it was one of the advertising managers from Chancery Lane wanting me to do an urgent favour for him. Within minutes we were discussing with the studio a possible creative design for an advertisement to appear in his publication. It was well into the afternoon before the ad was ready for presentation. However, on contacting the advertising manager, he rather hesitantly asked me to do him another favour. In view of the short time available he asked if we could deliver the advertisement to the advertiser for approval. Again I agreed but then realised that our messenger service had finished for the day so it was left to me to take it! Being the height of the rush hour, all the buses were full and there were no taxis available. I dashed through Lincoln Inn Fields into Kingsway and round the Aldwych till I reached the right address. Up a flight of stairs to a reception room where I was ushered into a tidy and bright office and introduced to a stockily built executive. He was expecting me and at once carefully scrutinized the copy and layout of the advertisement. As I was about to leave he started to talk about the possibilities of future promotions. I left his office late that evening but well rewarded. The press advertisement was accepted immediately and a sizeable amount of publicity requirements was ordered. Within twenty four hours I had learned yet more from the wonder of the Lord; Ted in his obedience and sensitivity to the Holy Spirit caused me to be thrown on to the Lord, resulting in Him providing an account worth more than five times that of Ted's business. The turnover accrued from this new account increased rapidly to become one of the largest held by our company during the time I worked there. I had also seen the wisdom of trusting and leaning fully upon the Lord in all things and upon His promises, and to avoid leaning on fellow Christians and using them as crutches in our daily living.

I was always anxious to share my new found faith and testimony when occasions arose and was provided with an interesting opportunity with another of our clients during one of my regular courtesy calls. The company was involved in the marine industry and situated by the busy waters of the Thames. My close encounter with a former naval officer, now a director of the company, was in his neat office overlooking the river where craft of all shapes and sizes were sailing up and down the Thames. My client appeared to be troubled with his telephone connections for as I entered the room he gave vent to his frustration by slamming the phone down on the receiver with a few choice words. As I sat patiently while he was still trying to contact his sales force, I started consoling his fruitless efforts by informing him of a number that was never engaged, always received an immediate reply and cost nothing! His rapid retort to my rather offbeat remark almost caught me off guard, but I was aware the Lord seemed to be guiding me each step of the way. 'And what kind of telephone directory do you have for a number like that?' The next few moments were intriguing as I elaborated on my first statement; opening my case I produced a Bible – my telephone directory.

At the time I never gave it a thought as to what part of the murky Thames I might have found myself in after this kind of remark! Opening the flimsy pages I turned the book round and invited him to read for himself the number I had in mind, it was long before STD had become fully operational! Jeremiah 33.3. He read it with some amusement, 'Call unto Me and I will answer you and show you great and mighty things which thou knowest not.'

The following hour was centred on his pointed question, 'How can you be a Christian in an advertising agency and how come you own a Bible?'

A somewhat potted presentation followed on my River Kwai experience which appeared to interest him, after which, we thought it time to get back to business. Soon afterwards I bid him farewell and left. The reason for the brief encounter became evident two weeks later when my client telephoned the office asking if I would be available one evening? I told him at once that I was free and wondered what he had in mind. It appeared that he was responsible for arranging guest speakers for their local Businessmen's Association. The speaker that was booked had been taken ill suddenly and, as he was to share his experiences in the Far East, my client thought it would be fitting to invite me in his place. I appreciated his invitation, but when I attempted to decline his offer, he became quite persistent, even when I hinted the message would have a fairly high spiritual theme. His reply was unexpected, 'It will be good for them to hear it!'

Preparing for an evening of this nature was quite different from a visit to a local church or mission hall! Over seventy businessmen were packed in a hotel suite ready to be entertained. I was more than relieved that the Lord was in control of this particular evening. One of my two business friends from the City had joined with me, and being a prayer warrior, I knew something was going to happen that evening. The entire period of the talk was noticeably silent until the vote of thanks, presented by a Jewish executive, was delivered. His comments were more than interesting, he continued, 'I do not think we have attended an evening dinner function like this before. It has been most enlightening and prompts me to say, when I think of my youth, that we businessmen seem to have drifted from the Good Book we were brought up on.'

It was some time before we could gauge the depth of the work accomplished that evening. Several spoke with Ted and me; however, eventually one person singled us out when he considered it safe to do so and spoke to us. As others were engaged at the bar, this person took no time in admitting what had been said was for him, how twenty years earlier he was a keen minister in an active church, but now, looking back, he realised he had left God out and was deeply discouraged. The Lord, in His goodness, ministered through us to this person. We were able to confirm to him what he already knew, although he thought it useless; that if he was willing to repent of his past misdeeds, and ask the Lord to forgive him and turn around with His grace and compassion the Lord would do just that! When the Lord forgives, He also forgets. He no longer remembers the matter, it is covered by the precious blood of Jesus. Some of us forgive on many occasions but it takes a long time, even forever, to forget.

11: Trusting the Lord

The years passed and the coming of commercial television brought another phase in the way the Lord was leading me day by day with interesting opportunities, confirming that it is possible to be a Christian in a commercial business whilst aiming to walk and live in the Spirit. I began to realise that the contents of the New Testament, particularly its many promises and words of encouragement, were an inspiration to me in home, church and other situations.

Several of the company's clients were naturally eager to be early participants in taking time in the newly launched Independent Television stations and I was delegated to an additional position as television executive, which brought me in contact with a variety of different people including clients and producers. In those early days, I often became involved in planning both live and filmed commercials. This meant that several hours would be spent in scripting, storyboard and presentation sessions in the London studios. I recall one instance, doing a 'dry run' for a domestic washing machine commercial, which was again to confirm how the Lord can reach others, particularly when I was learning to aim at being sensitive to the Holy Spirit. It is not until you decide to take each day at a time and keep your eyes upon the Lord, in meditating on the Scriptures and believing what one is reading, that this appears to come naturally without any striving. The visuals had been discussed and the storyboard agreed when the producer called a halt for a coffee break. During this time someone stumbled across a new film which was due for its trade showing in the West End that very week. The name of the film provided some interesting comments for the remainder of the break. It was entitled *The Bridge on the River Kwai*, and had been heavily promoted prior to its London première the coming week.

When the publicity representatives of the television company heard I was one of the many thousands in captivity on the railroad in Thailand, they refilled their coffee cups. The producer joined us and I gave him a brief résumé of my experience. Before we left the studio he fired a parting shot directly at me asking if I would be prepared to say a few words in front of the cameras! My immediate reply, without fully realising what I was saying, was 'I don't see why not,' and gave it little further thought. A month or so later the sequel to my earlier commitment came with a telephone call from a producer preparing material for a new religious television programme. He reminded me of my previous discussion with the commercial side of the company and indicated that he was to produce a programme to cover the Remembrance Day for that year. He had two participants, one an MP, the other a Methodist minister. He was looking for a third person who could speak on the subject of forgiveness.

The weeks which followed involved several meetings with the producer, where I fully appreciated how much time and energy was involved in preparing a programme lasting only thirty minutes. The day arrived and it meant a train journey to a large Midlands industrial city where I entered the large and formidable studios. I arrived just after two in the afternoon but found this was not too soon for the programme even though it was not being transmitted until six thirty pm. The hours leading up to the live transmission were spent in discussions running through the main topics of the programme, which gave us a good lead-in, as the transmission signals were being counted down. With three cameras, support technicians and control panel personnel all at the ready, the final moment had come and it was going out over the centre of the country. I must confess, the 'star' of the programme, as far as I was concerned, was certainly not me but the New Testament. Several times, as the book was referred to, cameras used tracking shots into close-ups of God's living word, and I was able to share and confirm the reality of the living word.

Most of us individuals in the large and somewhat cold world of commerce, wonder how to try and better ourselves, in which direction to aim and particularly if one is a Christian, how to fit all this in with what one reads in the living book. We are so often in a hurry, trying to manoeuvre situations before the time. The more I have considered this problem in every day living, the more I am convinced that the best remedy comes in Proverbs 16.3, which is so simple yet so hard to accept: 'Commit your works unto the Lord and thy thoughts shall be established'. I am certain that we have very little reason to try working everything out, or getting into a panic, when if we put everything, every day, in His hands, our day is directed in peace, regardless of any turmoil around us. Each day, as you live with expectancy, with the Lord in control, is another day in which you learn a little more of how real He is.

In the advertising world there are many functions arranged by publishers and the media, who are intent on reaching the advertisers and their agents. Along with thirty others I was invited by a well known publisher, not to a dinner or show but to attend a cricket match. I had little interest in this sport but the day turned out to be fine and sunny so I decided to make the most of it. Arriving at the ground near St John's Wood in London, I found a 'Gentlemen v Players' match in progress. No sooner had I selected a seat amidst numerous advertising personnel when I found I had a good vantage point and began to relax for the next five or six hours. Within a short time a smartly dressed waiter approached asking for my drinks order, which was promptly brought. The person sitting next to me also was given a drink and to my surprise it was the very same as mine – iced orange juice. They were the only soft drinks on the tray and as we both accepted our drinks we looked at each other with a knowing smile. This was the Lord's way of breaking the 'ice' with us, as we soon realised we had something very much in common.

It is often noticeable that when you meet another believer for the first time, a total stranger, you sense you have known each other for years – this is one of the many attributes which the Christian message confirms. It was several years later, when operating my own advertising company, that my cricketing companion telephoned me to say he was in a position to spend a substantial amount on publicity and was I interested?

Moving and living a day at a time is by far the best way, as I found to my advantage in the timing of this commission which resulted in handling the publicity for a well known communications company. Strange how the Lord can even use a soft drink to accomplish His connections for us! Not only did we meet for business promotions but often enjoyed fellowship in London, Farnborough, Frankfurt and other venues where my colleague's company were exhibiting.

During those thirteen years working for an expanding advertising agency, representatives used to call in the hope of obtaining business from our clients. Many times in discussions, during coffee breaks, the business representatives from the media around Fleet Street would call and soon become engrossed in the reasons why we should use their publication for our clients.

On many occasions it was amazing to witness how, after some of these reps had finally tried to 'sell' new areas in the media field to me, I found myself 'selling' what turned out later to be the best product on the market! More than once a rep, once full of enthusiasm, had returned months later to share his disillusionment on being made redundant. One, I remember, returning from a holiday, found a dismissal letter waiting for him on his desk. Many times I witnessed this happening to ordinary men, who felt they were set up for life. They would sense that I and other Christians had found the answer in the living Lord and His word.

By this time I felt it was time to launch out and operate my own business – after all, the temptation is great when you are on the other side to the management. It came in a different way from which I had planned.

Starting my own advertising and PR consultancy was a move of my own undertaking and from the very lengthy period before work materialised, I admit I was probably going one step ahead, instead of waiting for the Lord's leading in such an important matter. During the first year a little encouragement came when thinking about a change of office from the Fleet Street area out towards Woodford or Chingford. One morning, while my car was being serviced, a car pulled up abruptly alongside a bus stop where I had been standing. A curt voice from within the car asked if I wanted a lift to the station some three miles away. In all the years since the war I had never been offered a lift by a stranger. I accepted his kind gesture –

after all this was much more comfortable than a bus. By the time we arrived at the underground station at Walthamstow, not only was I thankful for the lift but also for the fact that I had now been offered business premises in Woodford. The stranger, who I never saw again, was an estate agent and with the information he gave me, I was able to move into new offices the following week. How well timed are God's answers to our problems, yet not always the way or avenue in which we think they will be accomplished. A week before I had never imagined a passing motorist might stop and offer me an office at the right price, yet here I was fully installed in my own offices.

The first year was far from encouraging; my bank balance was the opposite of what I had considered it should be! I had no contacts, and was prohibited by the previous employers from obtaining business from the clients with whom I had, in most cases, excellent relationships. But I struggled on, and struggled was the operative word. The Lord had to show me how He moves when the time is right, especially in critical situations. Had I stepped out at the wrong time? Where were all the friendly reps who gave some wonderful promises of new work? It is at times like these that Satan moves in for an onslaught if we are not careful and, if we allow any opening for him, he will enter like a flood. But, the Lord was so gracious and concerned for me. I realised my failure in my own way of running things and I decided to ask His forgiveness: I was once more on my knees.

I began to put myself right, and admitted that somewhere along the way I had been going adrift, depending on others or important people, as well as my own ego of being a proud owner of a company! Opening my Bible, my eyes focused on these very direct words, 'Call upon Me in the day of trouble; I will deliver thee and thou shalt glorify

Me'. As I pondered these words I knew that if, as in previous cases, the Lord was saying something, He really meant what He said and I had to believe it! I did just that and at that moment I sincerely thanked the Lord for those firm but comforting words as if I was replying, saying in my heart, 'Thank you Lord, this is a day of trouble today, and I am calling upon you and I know you will deliver me somehow in this situation.' Looking back at it from a cold calculated business point of view, there was hardly enough credit in the bank to draw on for petty cash, it was that bad. But the moment I thanked the Lord and believed His word and claimed it as His promise and condition to me, all fear immediately left me; it was as if a curtain was lifted. Again, in the cold light of day, I needed a sizeable cash injection within a week or two or I would be back to the jungles of Fleet Street looking for a job. Whilst there was no immediately apparent miracle, each of the following days passed with a feeling of peace, that all was well: this assurance never left me. It was evidence of the faith that had many times been given by the Lord in His graciousness and that had borne us through when it seemed impossible – right from the time He revealed the day of freedom from the camp near to the Kwai. I really get excited, which may seem strange for an adman to say, when I know that Jesus Christ is the same, yesterday, today and forever.

It must have been five days later before anything out of the ordinary seemed to happen. One of the Fleet Street reps I had met some years ago and whom I had in a small way been able to help spiritually, gave me a call, asking me to contact a central heating firm based in South London; they were requiring help in launching their new products to the UK market. Repeatedly, I tried to make contact with the manager and for reasons I could not understand, never got through. A day or so later my rep colleague again contacted me to tell me this company was waiting to see me. It took several hours before I was able to make direct contact on the telephone. The next day I found myself in a lengthy meeting which brought about something that rarely happens in the advertising business, or in any other business. The company were most apologetic in asking me to do the near-impossible as far as timing was concerned. Within a few days, following market research, the media and creative planning of the campaign was presented and approved. Every part of the artwork and design through to back-up literature was approved. The complete campaign was launched and well in hand within three weeks of conception. And within seven days all bills were paid showing their appreciation for the work undertaken. Once again I found myself thanking the Lord for His deliverance and the business began to run in the way we should have started a year earlier! How different life can be without the striving and the struggling when we decide to wait upon Him. For nearly twenty years our business continued, with numerous opportunities in Christian testimony to both clients and media reps alike. Through all the years, where we have gone through the fire, we have never burned, and never drowned in deep waters. We can say with confidence, even though we fail at times to keep in touch with Him, the Lord has never failed us, has always met our needs and according to His living word, we know that He will *never* fail.

12: Should the Church use Modern Methods of Communications?

Full involvement as a Christian in the world of publicity can lead to churches, missions and societies seeking expert advice and assistance in the use of modern media communications. Following the overall success of the London Crusade, many evangelists and churchmen gave second thoughts to the possibility of considering the use of publicity within their own particular field. As many have since indicated, the timing and the preparation, with the combined efforts of the many prayer groups across the country and the selective use of the mass media for the Crusade at Harringay was, without a doubt, an effective and worthwhile attack launched to reach the greater part of the City. As a Christian adman I have often been challenged on this important and inviting subject by Christian businessmen of various denominations when faced with the opportunity of committing themselves and their churches to high budget spending in promotions aimed at increasing their congregations. My reply is very simple: unless the Lord gives a direct confirmation to any of us in this position, then it could be a somewhat fruitless effort. Whatever the Holy Spirit is directing, when any of us are in a position of indecision, the answer will be given if one is waiting upon the Lord; each situation is always different from the other. For the Greater London

Crusade, for example, the type of publicity produced was not the same as for any other Crusade. On numerous occasions the most successful evangelistic ventures stem from a prayerfully co-ordinated base by the planners. There is no reason why the Christian Church should not engage in the modern age of communications covering satellites, cable, provincial and national television. Use of the press, with the best presentation in design and copy for literature, can carry the instant message of hope and salvation. On this important subject of communications, many Christians are aware of the way in which the persecuted Church in many overseas countries have to depend not upon the printed word to advertise the gatherings but on the Holy Spirit to direct. In the unique revivals of this century, encouraging reports from remote parts of the world indicate how the Holy Spirit has been the channel through which countless thousands have been reached for Jesus Christ. Being somewhat dependent on advertising myself, it is not difficult to become enthusiastic when considering an advertising campaign. In the natural, with one's experience in the marketing world, one has to watch for the subtleties as against the spiritual reality. The final results tell the story, often too late, with disappointing spiritual activity and far from satisfactory financial returns to cover the basic costs. In moments like these, I am so thankful for being continually reminded of the living word and my need for complete dependence on it for every circumstance and situation.

It has been a privilege to meet and work with a number of Christian Societies during the period 1954–1974, experiencing positive and lasting results as I observed how they proved a continual walk of faith in their daily tasks.

A remarkable encounter in this direction came only a few months after my return from the jungles. I was walking towards St Paul's Cathedral, when my eyes were attracted to an outstanding window display. It was a large map of South East Asia dominated by the centrepiece highlighting Thailand. Unaware of who the owners of the bookshop might be, I cautiously entered the shop which was filled with excellent displays of books covering missionary activities mixed with a galaxy of Bibles of different sizes and colours. I was met with a smile of welcome from the sales assistant who informed me the shop was part of the Christian Literature Crusade. It was not long before I realised she was more than the usual type of sales girl, particularly as she was well versed on the statistics of South East Asia. Some years later I heard that she had gone to India as a missionary with WEC – Worldwide Evangelization Crusade.

Little did I realise then that I would, at a much later date, be invited by WEC to address one of their missionary seminars. My brief was to advise on approach methods to the media, making effective contact with the local and national media throughout the country. Many of the delegates were missionaries home on furlough and they formed a wide selection of personalities when it came to question time. It is strange how a carefully prepared presentation can be changed during the period of your talk. The Lord did this very thing to me: I was following my usual commercial approach on how to negotiate with editors of papers, the ethics of aiming for good public relations, encouraging many workers that they may well be in possession of exciting stories, when my line of delivery seemed to change. A question was posed by one of my close associates within the Mission, which provided an amazing turnround. Within a few moments I found I was advocating that the best and lasting way to reach the media effectively would be through intercessory prayer. From this direction, we could accomplish far greater results with more effective contacts than most of us would ever achieve by using our own strength. I had no idea that my own presentation was going to terminate in a direct call to prayer. I realised that the WEC Missionary Organisation needed no encouragement from me in this direction, knowing how the Lord had blessed their work for many years. Their dependence, as with many other faith missions, upon the Lord is clear, the annual balance sheets providing a telling story: there are no desperate pleas for finance to meet the needs of the Crusade and its many workers both at home and overseas. Personal encounters of this nature began to add the vital ingredients towards the enriching of one's testimony, confirming the word of the Lord, without a doubt, to be so true. . . 'My God shall supply all your needs, according to His riches in glory, by Christ Jesus. . .'

Another incident from which I was to learn much about being careful in the use of media for Christian work came when I was invited to attend a publicity committee for the visit of a well-loved American evangelist, whose ministry excelled towards teenagers throughout the world. It was the final week of meetings across the country, with a large rally in London to be followed by several gatherings in the West Country. A radio interview provided interesting coverage nationally; it also, however, attracted a TV researcher. Within hours of the radio broadcast, the evangelist's book had been hurriedly read by a member of the TV company. Everything was remarkably rapid and before half the day was completed, the evangelist, a member of the committee and myself were on the platform at Paddington station looking for an empty compartment, when we were confronted by the TV producers, researchers and numerous camera crew and sound units. We were informed that they had arranged for two compartments to be reserved for our trip! Some thirty minutes later, with the initial shock wearing off, our train slid out across the network of rails into the evening sunshine. As we sped past Slough we realised the journey was going to be far from restful. Interviews were recorded and filmed, for the most part to be featured in a new series of documentaries. By being involved in three days of close liaison with the production crew it seemed to us at the time of shooting to be an interesting production. Several months later we were to view the edited thirty minute programme. As many of our friends at the time recalled, the result of the eagerly awaited programme was very disappointing from the Crusade's angle; and from that period, I have advised great caution when being approached by the media.

As with every day situations, we need at all times to be open to the Holy Spirit and not expect the same result each time.

One other presentation on television did however turn out to be successful. That time I was replying to a telephone call in my office, when I realised it was a researcher for another TV programme. The lady in question was trying to locate a minister for a Sunday night programme. The minister, whom I knew, was unfortunately out of the country and, whilst disappointed, she became a little more persistent in enquiring if I knew of any possible alternatives. I was able to give her the name of an Anglican minister, the Rev. Trevor Dearing, who lived nearby in Ilford and who was being greatly used in the ministry of salvation, combined with healing and deliverance. A live transmission was arranged for the following weekend, with many prominent people taking part. The subject centred around the occult, and healing. Trevor Dearing took a prominent part in the programme and the presenters who were more than pleased with the result, suggested that he should be given more 'air' time at a later date. The later date turned out to be the following week. It was also a live transmission. Many Christians prayed for the Sunday evening; the programme revolved around the controversial subject of healing and aroused great interest from viewers. Following the close of the transmission a caption board was displayed several times during the late evening, advising viewers to contact Trevor Dearing direct for any information. The studio switchboards were jammed with calls.

The outcome of that telephone call for a minister to take part in a discussion programme, was very encouraging, a church mission hall in Birmingham was booked for several consecutive nights to answer questions put by viewers. Each night the church was packed to the doors. Trevor spent over an hour explaining to the hundreds eagerly seeking healing who was actually the Healer.

He and the workers at the mission had the marvellous opportunity of telling how Jesus Christ is the answer to every problem in their lives. Later each evening Trevor ministered to the sick, lame and infirm. This was a remarkable testimony of how the Lord moved through one telephone call to obtain the person required of the Lord for the programme, and of those who prayed faithfully for Trevor. This all led to around 1,200 persons responding to a personal invitation to take Jesus Christ as their own personal Saviour thus transforming their lives. Beyond this many were healed by a touch from the divine Physician during those few days. It is because of situations like this, interwoven with other less positive results, that I refrain from being dogmatic on issues concerning the use of modern communications but in each area encourage others to seek the Lord for His direction.

13: A Shadow of the Past – From Japan

It is said that time is a healer. In some cases that may be true but I am not sure that is so for many of the prisoners of war who returned from the hell camps of South East Asia. Nearly forty years later, one comes across certain survivors of the tragic years of the war who are suffering, not only physically but mentally, taunted by painful memories. I consider myself fortunate and am more than thankful to God for health in every way and for His mighty saving and keeping power. I am so thankful that, following my Christian experiences so soon after my release, all personal bitterness, hatred and malice towards our captors appeared to go; and I might add, this was in no way by my own efforts – it could only be a power given from the forgiving Creator, as clearly indicated in the Bible.

Until the sixties I had not been confronted with anyone from Japan, but then a very important incident suddenly occurred. One morning, whilst I was still engaged with the Fleet Street advertising agency, the Director of the Pocket Testament League telephoned me from their North London headquarters, enquiring if I would be able to assist in press and public relations for their society. He was aware of my professional abilities but perhaps more interested in the knowledge that I had been a prisoner of war under the Japanese and had subsequently come into a Christian faith. The request was surprising. I was invited to assist in handling the forthcoming visit of a Japanese

Christian to the UK and my pride in showing that I bore no malice against the Japanese was to be tested. This was a great challenge, as I thought an encounter like this would never occur! I had no intention of ever again visiting any Oriental countries, much less of coming face to face with any Japanese.

The Pocket Testament League carry out an excellent work in providing portions of Scriptures to many countries throughout the world and I am constantly reminded that, had it not been for the Word of God, I would not have been delivered from the Kwai in such a remarkable way! These thoughts soon registered and confirmed that I should accept the request.

The day duly arrived and it involved a visit to Heathrow, one of the world's busiest airports. Several newsmen from Fleet Street hovered around the arrivals lounge in Terminal Two waiting for the flight from Holland. The reality of this particular job was now dawning on me. Here I was waiting to meet a visitor due to step from the immigration area at any moment. I couldn't help wondering what my immediate reaction was going to be – how was I going to face this problem after all these years and prove not only to myself but to others, how real my testimony was. Many times I had witnessed to others that only Jesus Christ was the answer, when we in our own strength cannot embrace or even contemplate love for our enemies. My mixed thoughts and emotions were quickly dispelled as camera laden reporters suddenly sprang into action, their equipment flashing and clicking at the appearance of the Japanese personality. The newsmen, endeavouring to obtain the best shots, delayed the moment of greeting anxiously awaited by the reception party. Here he was: as I stepped towards him it was the last person with whom I had ever expected to come face to face! My mind raced back to the crowded ship where I first heard the news that Pearl Harbor had been attacked. Little did I ever realise that I would be confronted eye to eye with the very leader who caused so much havoc on that vivid morning of 7th December 1941 – the former Japanese Commander, who by that famous attack had plunged Japan into the war with America at Pearl Harbor, Captain Mitsuo Fuchida! Captain Fuchida was en route to the United States, stopping off for a few days in Britain as guest of the Pocket Testament League. He had become the Japanese Representative for the PTL soon after his amazing conversion to the Christian faith. Following the rapid but in-depth interrogation by the reporters who had encircled him, we made our way back to London and the offices of the PTL. This was my first encounter with a Japanese person and it had to be someone of this calibre. Up until this time there was little direct trading from the UK with Japan and the media were wondering why he had decided to visit our country. The more I considered my own feelings, and the feelings of other ex-prisoner friends of mine who had been less fortunate, the more I gradually became aware of a peaceful tranquillity passing through my whole being. This inner peace is hard to explain and convey to anyone else: it needs to be experienced. I can only suggest it was the same peace which swept into me the moment I accepted Jesus Christ as my Saviour in far away Rangoon. The bitter hatred, the natural horror compounded with fear, which I half-expected, half-dreaded were simply not there. The apprehension was gone, and it was without doubt not of my doing. I was more than thankful as it confirmed once again that Jesus was right in what He said in His word. As I was still struggling privately to weigh up my situation in the modern world of commerce, trying to analyse the full meaning of forgiveness when put to the test, the compassion of the Lord was far stronger, showing me His love could never be manufactured by anyone in their own strength. Captain Fuchida's first words to me when he was introduced to me and told of my captivity were memorable. They were words full of sadness, remorse and a sincere concern for all my friends and the thousands who had suffered so tragically during the conflict. He asked for forgiveness and apologised for the way in which certain orders by the Japanese authorities had been given. Moved by his open sincerity, I almost felt sorry for him, and the picture came to mind of the thief who was hanging on the cross beside Jesus those two thousand years ago asking to be forgiven and remembered. How then could I be unforgiving when the Lord Jesus had shed his blood to forgive *me?*

During his stay in London we shared in a number of evangelistic meetings. Captain Fuchida's testimony, which he related to me both personally and which I heard during the meetings, was in a strange and unique way involved with another former POW, in the Far East Jacob DeShazer. He continued to tell me of the most amazing stories of a US Sergeant who, during the early years of the war, flew as a member of General Jimmie Doolittle's Squadron on the first raid over Japan in April 1942. As with many in battle at that time, he had a bitter hatred for the people of Japan, for what they had done at Pearl Harbor. Through an unfortunate turn of events the aircraft ran short of fuel resulting in the crew bailing out into Japanese-held territory in China. Soon they were captured, and his bitterness grew more intense. They were eventually shipped to Tokyo where they were imprisoned, beaten, half-starved and put in solitary confinement. They were moved from prisons in Shanghai, Nanking and Peiping. There, three of his comrades were executed and some months later another of his friends died of slow starvation. Hatred grew in him and built up into a frenzy at the hopeless position he found himself in. He could not imagine hating his captors more. His thoughts began to follow lines similar to those I had come to consider during my captivity. Why such hatred? Why wars? Where was it all leading? It was during a long term in solitary confinement that he turned towards Christianity and considered that perhaps here was a way of changing this awful bitterness. He was overcome with an inexplicable but persistent desire to examine the Bible, to see for himself if he could find the secret. But he had great difficulty in getting a Bible from his captors. However in May 1944, a Japanese guard eventually produced a Bible and, throwing it into his cell, informed him he could only keep it for three weeks. Eagerly during those weeks he read each page, chapter after chapter, book after book. It began to grip his heart as he read on. The more he read the more enthralled he became until he found he was reading the greatest story ever told. Searching through the books of the prophets he discovered the Scriptures were continually focusing on the promise of a divine redeemer from sin. Reading on into the New Testament, he was thrilled to discover in the record of the birth of Jesus, the fulfilment of the prophecies contained in the books of Isaiah, Jeremiah, Micah and others. It was in June 1944 that at last his eyes were opened to the truth contained in the word of God. But what is remarkable to me is that he called upon the Lord in Japan, during the same month of the same year that I also called to the Lord whilst in Thailand. Many hundreds of miles apart, each of us without a padre, pastor, minister or a fellow-Christian anywhere near, yet the word of God, anointed by the Holy Spirit, was sufficiently powerful to bring the truth to us almost simultaneously. He began to see the Japanese in a different way as if the Lord was opening new spiritual eyes, even though he was so badly starved and beaten. Those words of Jesus came alive to him, 'Father, forgive them for they know not what they do.' He began to pray for the Lord to forgive his torturers. During his final years in captivity, whilst only the memories of the Scriptures remained in his mind and heart, he became very ill. Recalling his friend's death by starvation two years previously he felt perhaps he was going the same way. For several days the guards took opportunities to beat him severely, leaving him to fade away in despair. It was then that God intervened and strengthened him to endure this suffering. Freedom came to the Sergeant, Jacob DeShazer, as for me, on that unforgettable day in August 1945.

But a more remarkable thing was to happen. Shortly after his return to the United States he became aware that the Lord was showing him he ought to become a missionary. Following a few years at training college he eventually went to the country of God's calling – Japan! Captain Fuchida understood he was still there when he left Japan for this tour.

As Captain Fuchida continued, he shared with me what had happened to him since that momentous day when he lead the raid on Pearl Harbor. He said that he was the first and the last person to be over the target, after personally sinking the battleship *Maryland*. He was the sole surviving officer of the seven commanders and thirty two squadron leaders whom he had led into the raid. He felt that God had spared his life so that he might become a Christian. He had had many close brushes with death including six crashes at sea. Shortly before the battle for Midway he underwent an appendectomy on board ship.

Though he did not fly, he was in the thick of the battle nevertheless. A direct hit on the ship broke both his legs and hurled him overboard. He was rescued and was sent back to Japan. Had he not been out of action he would have commanded the Japanese air force at Guadalcanal and might well have met the same fate as many of his fellow officers who died there.

After the war, with twenty five years of service behind him, he retired and took up farming, but it was a path of thorns to him. During the post war years he began to realise the unreliability of other men. He built himself a house and, as he pondered on his life, his mind was gradually being led to think of the presence of God, the Creator of all. He began to feel ashamed of his former godless idea that man's own power and ability was his only trustworthy resource. As the years of the war began to recede further into the distance, nations throughout the world talked of peace. He shared how he felt the only way for Japan to survive and prosper, would be for the Japanese people to become thoroughly peaceful, and peace-loving. One day at the large Shibuya Rail Station in Tokyo, Captain Fuchida was given a Christian pamphlet written by none other than Sgt Jacob DeShazer, and entitled *I was a Prisoner of Japan*. Immediately he was captivated and read every word with great enthusiasm.

One paragraph particularly interested Fuchida: it was the description of Jacob's strong desire to read the Bible during his imprisonment. He recalled to mind what he had heard before, that Christianity could transform human hatred to true brotherly love. After reading the leaflet he too felt compelled to purchase a Bible. This he quickly did. Before he had read many pages his mind was strongly impressed and captivated. 'This is it!' he was convinced. His initial reaction to all that he had been

116

reading was first of all to become a good Christian. Opening his heart and whole life he accepted Jesus Christ as his personal Saviour on April 14th 1950. He, an ex-officer of the Japanese military and I, an ex-prisoner of a Japanese war-camp, shared and discussed a number of incidents which happened in our lives operating as it were from completely different sides of the world, and came to the conclusion that men of all nations can come together in real fellowship and lasting friendship when we become brothers in Jesus Christ, and make Him Lord in our lives.

When he left for America a week later, he shared his great desire for a deeper understanding of God's word and told how reading the Bible every day and experiencing the anointing of the Holy Spirit, brought a complete peace and lasting joy he had never before believed existed. After his visit I was so thankful that I too had found the only way to change my life. As it was for Jacob DeShazer, I too had been provided with a channel of supernatural love for my former enemies.

Some years later Captain Fuchida was invited to be a technical adviser for an American film unit making an epic to be distributed worldwide. Entitled *Tora, Tora, Tora,* the film depicted the full story of the Pearl Harbor raid. A few years later, whilst still engaged in evangelistic work in the USA and Japan, the Lord took Mitsuo Fuchida into His presence.

During the many years since my release, I have met a number of people who have been associated with the Kwai. Recalling a time when addressing an evening evangelistic dinner near Blackpool, organised by the local Chapter of the Full Gospel Business Men's Fellowship, I noticed one gentleman at the front table who I thought had become nervous, and seemed relieved when I had finished. His need to light a cigarette gave me the opportunity to speak to him. I had made a comment that if there were any RAF personnel who may have been engaged in operations in the South East Asia Command, I would look forward to having 'fellowship' with them at the end of the meeting. This rather nervous gentleman was one such airman who was sent on the bombing raids up and down the line and hesitantly admitted this whilst still clutching his cigarette. Even in circumstances such as these I was able to share a little of the love of God with this man who had listened intently during the evening.

One other encouraging appointment came whilst taking part in the FGBMFI Convention in Scotland in 1981. The main speaker was a retired American Colonel of the USAAF, now a servant of God, one time fighter pilot, Colonel Heath Bottomly, who had served in three theatres of war from the close of World War II through to Korea and other SE Asian areas. Having heard my testimony during the breakfast session, I was amused to hear him admit to being another of those responsible for the Kwai Bridge attacks. His testimony is another which tells of the amazing way that men who, before the war, had not the slightest thought of God, came out of those dark days into a glorious light. This can only come about as we take God at His Word, believing everything He says – and letting Him make a far better job of our lives thereafter.

14: Renewal in Fleet Street

Five years had elapsed since the close of the London Crusade at Harringay, churches in many parts of the country having benefited from the three month long Crusade. More than once I heard it suggested that the Crusade should have continued but, in one sense, I don't think it ever really stopped.

Throughout the country signs of a growing desire for something deeper in the Christian life and experience were beginning to appear, not everywhere at once but it was noticeable that a work of the Holy Spirit was emerging. This was not confined to any one particular church, fellowship or denomination. In various areas, some churchgoers were taking a greater interest in reading the Bible. In others, efforts were made to support local fellowship prayer groups which had been running at a low ebb. At the same time, a vision was beginning to surface for outreach activities, and a new compassion stirred for other Christians wherever they worshipped, and for those who did not know the Lord. During this initial awakening, something interesting was starting in a small way within the heart of media land. Fleet Street, noisily situated in the heart of London, is not exactly where one would expect something of a spiritual nature to be generated.

The Fleet Street movement of the Holy Spirit originated a mile or so from the heart of the newspaper industry in the YMCA building in Tottenham Court Road. For a year or so I had been handling publicity for the Home Missions Department of the Assemblies of God in Great Britain & Ireland and it was through this contact that I found myself a regular visitor to a monthly evening fellowship and meal at the YMCA. About seventy of us would meet, mostly businessmen, and including several pastors and evangelists, and we sought ways in which to share the Gospel throughout the country by modern techniques.

However, the months slipped by and whilst there were always plenty of good ideas, we did not seem to get them into operation in any definite way.

However, one evening a pastor from one of the churches in South London, rose to his feet and suggested that maybe, after a year, it was about time we listened to God, rather than tell Him what we wanted to do. This man put his finger right on the problem and, like all good pastors, offered a very simple and encouraging solution.

He suggested that as most of those present were businessmen who worked in the City, why not start a regular lunchtime prayer meeting in the heart of the City! The idea was received with enthusiasm, although I treated it with the same caution as any market research suggestion. To me the idea of a prayer meeting was a place for elderly ladies once a week in the local church, or at best, a therapy for more spiritually minded men than myself. Prior to this period, I had met two businessmen during my course of work in Fleet Street. One, Frank Birkenshaw, the other, Jim Rattenbury, both of whom turned out to be lasting friends through all the succeeding years. Frank, who worked with a large Christian Publishers off Ludgate Hill, had a great love of Gospel music and attended an Elim Church near Clapham. He was a supporter at the monthly evening meetings in the YMCA and was greatly respected for his printing and presentation skills. In fact, I recall those early days when some of his original ideas for layout and presentation were the basis for one of the new regular monthly Christian glossy magazines. He was Pentecostal and it was some months before I fully appreciated the wide range of denominations that existed. However I was soon to learn quickly with some illuminating results. Frank was as keen with his prayer life as he was gifted with his printing skills.

He telephoned me a week after the YMCA meeting informing me that a location for our prayer meeting had been found, right on our doorstep in Fleet Street. A room had been booked in the St Bride's Institute for the following Thursday and he was hoping to see me there. The day arrived. Lunchtime came but I had conveniently arranged another lunch appointment in haste (and perhaps with a small measure of quiet panic). Later in the afternoon Frank called me wondering if I was alright. His call, although gentle in approach, convicted me. I knew in my heart I should have joined the others. Fortunately for me Frank persisted: on the day before the next week's meeting, he called 'just to remind me' – this time I knew I had to accept, and I did. I began to think quickly. I'd heard a few stories of these other denominations and was already getting cold feet. However, a bright idea came my way. Jim Rattenbury, my other newly found friend, also in the print business, was coming my way that Thursday morning. I knew he often spoke about the occasions he had experienced of the Lord answering prayer in many practical ways. He had even been healed, he told me. I decided I would invite him to go to the prayer meeting with me.

Strolling down Chancery Lane into Fleet Street we mingled with the lunch hour crowds. St Paul's Cathedral, at the top of Ludgate Hill, glistened in the midday sun. Jim and I were very much engrossed in an important matter which concerned us both and somehow we could not seem to reach an amicable solution as we approached St Bride's Institute. Climbing the steps we eventually found a small room on the upper floor; by this time we realised we'd have to forego any further discussion or decision relating to our problem until after the meeting. As we slipped into the small room we observed six or seven people praying, heads bowed. Taking our seats we listened with interest, for this turned out to be no ordinary prayer meeting. Somehow it was very much alive, even with so few in attendance there was an air of expectancy – a feeling of uplift to one's own senses. Evidently one of the ladies was deeply concerned for the many in Fleet Street who were bound for a lost eternity unless they repented. Her prayer of intercession was certainly from the heart, reaching to the Saviour – and I felt the desire of her prayer was not far off it's target. Those engaged in prayer were so sincere and made me realise they were in touch with the living God. For a little over an hour Jim and I relaxed in the atmosphere which was not only overwhelming but full of inexpressible joy. Eventually we had to leave before the meeting ended and as I was about to open the door, Jim held me gently by the arm, indicating I should remain for a moment.

One person was praying loudly and the remainder of the group were listening intently – but the prayer was certainly not in English. Almost as soon as the prayer finished it was followed by another, this time in English. Not only was the prayer loud and clear but the content shattered both Jim and me, I couldn't get out of the door quick enough to express my amazement to him. As we left the Institute Jim, who had spent many years in study of the Bible, ministry, church history and prophecy, told me that we had just heard a prophetic word. He explained that it came from the anointing of the Holy Spirit, with an interpretation following in English. Events like this caused me to search out for myself from the Bible any reference to this strange phenomenon – the gifts of the Holy Spirit. However, what was more remarkable was the content of the message. It contained, with precision, and direction, the answer to the very problem Jim and I had been troubled with on the way to that meeting. No one knew the problem except us and the Lord. That word from God was for us, and the answer it gave us was one which we could not possibly have worked out ourselves.

Each week Jim and I visited the prayer meeting and each week the numbers grew. We continued to meet for a little over three years and grew in size until the authorities of the Institute allowed us to move into the large, distinguished boardroom. A number of interesting points are worth noting. There was no particular organiser or leader for the gatherings. No one ever needed to address the meetings. We waited on the Lord, listened to His voice, and the prayers were exacting and brief requests, each within a continuity of the other intercessors. During those years the awe-inspiring awareness of the Lord was within our midst. In fact we would think carefully before engaging in prayer unless led of the Lord. Visitors to the meetings gave up their entire lunch break, in order not to miss what the Lord was sharing with us. Many young people, just starting work in the City, had this same thought in mind.

Each week they came, businessmen and women, young and old, ministers, vicars, evangelists, members of the press, secular as well as Christian. Other visitors came from Europe, America, Canada, Argentina, South Africa, the Far East and Japan. Many returned to their churches and fellowships with a desire to share what the Lord was doing in our midst. The outworking of this could be summed up in a deeper awareness of the Lord when in prayer, the Bible becoming an 'open book', a sincere love for other Christians whatever denomination, and the burning desire to reach the lost.

On several occasions we were not aware of the actual individuals visiting. However, many of us will long remember a visit from a lady missionary who, while home on furlough, visited the meeting and requested prayer for her return to the Congo in 1961. Several prayed for her and the anointing of the Holy Spirit was very evident. She returned to the Congo but never returned to Britain again. After capture by the rebels she lived out an amazing testimony under the hand of the Lord for nearly three years: Winnie Davies was killed by Congolese rebels just prior to release by Government soldiers on May 31st 1967.

A number of churches of various denominations were experiencing a new encouragement within their weekly services at this time and prayer meetings were beginning to find an increase in supporters. Worship and praise, as mentioned many times in the Old Testament, were being given their place within the evening services. From America came numerous requests for information concerning the renewal in parts of Britain. A strange request came to us during the autumn of 1965 when several of those connected with the Fleet Street meeting were asked if we could arrange a 'steering committee' for a group of Americans for a suggested visit to Britain in November. At that time several of us were sceptical of Americans and much of their high pressure presentations. After considerable persuasion several of us formed a committee and made the arrangements for a visit from a group calling themselves the Full Gospel Business Men's Fellowship International. It turned out to be another arm of evangelism aimed at business people and had been founded in 1952 by Demos Shakarian, a successful dairy farmer resident in Southern California. Demos was given guidance by inspiration of the Holy Spirit, for a unique new avenue of ministry, to reach men. Not through a preacher but through the testimony of the local plumber, dentist, salesman or other businessman. Hiring a café in Los Angeles he started with one or two meetings. Initially, they missed the mark, but within a year the Lord opened up avenues in a unique way, as it is recorded in his personal story entitled *The Happiest People on Earth*. Today over 2,600 groups throughout the world are holding monthly meetings for businessmen. God gave Demos a vision many years ago, which culminated in him seeing millions of men with heads raised, eyes that shone with joy, and hands lifted towards heaven. Men who in the past had been so isolated, now appeared to be linked together in a mutual love for God. The outcome of the steering committee opened up many opportunities for ministers, evangelists, businessmen and others to come together with expectancy for a two week period.

In handling the public relations for this visit, I recall an amusing episode which was related to me at a later date. Three Boeing 707s were chartered to fly the businessmen and their wives to Britain. At 33,000 feet over the Atlantic an irregularity was detected in one of the aircraft. There was no visible engineering or hydraulic reason for the fault and both pilot and co-pilot were baffled. They asked the flight engineer to take a quick check at the rear of the plane. As with all 707s they are rather long but not as wide as the more modern 747s. As the engineer began to walk along the carpeted gangway he was surprised to see no one

125

in any of the passenger seats in the forward section. Reaching the rear section he found all the passengers, not asleep but gathered together in praise and worship, preparing eagerly for their London visit! The flight engineer politely ordered them back to their original seats or they might meet their Maker sooner than envisaged!

The first week's itinerary included meetings for visitors from around London and the country in most of the main buildings in town including the Hilton, Westminster Chapel, the Metropolitan Tabernacle and the Royal Albert Hall. The initial impact was incredible, resulting in the first Chapters, as they are entitled, being established in Belfast, Preston and Cheshire. Over 170 Chapters are now fully operational in the UK and Ireland, with ministry directed to business men through regular breakfasts, luncheons or dinner functions with speakers.

During the period of the 'Fleet Street Prayer Meetings' one was equally aware and encouraged by simultaneous movements being created by the Holy Spirit throughout Britain, including such associations as The Fountain Trust, Intercessors for Britain, Youth with a Mission, the Lydia Fellowship, Nights of Prayer for Revival, FGBMFI, Women Aglow, City of London Luncheon Fellowships, and many others operating through Christian Unions in various industries. Some years later a group was launched under the direction of Rev. Trevor Dearing with the self explanatory title of 'Power, Praise and Healing Mission'. The team and Mission was formed following several years of Trevor Dearing's successful ministry in an East London Parish Church, near Ilford. Many churches around the country benefited from the visits of Trevor and his team, and many came to know the Lord through His healing touch upon them.

It is encouraging over the years to see the gradual

increase in the numbers of Christians around the country, many of whom began their Christian life during that era, whether it was at the first of Dr. Billy Graham's Crusades, the outpouring of the Holy Spirit during the Fleet Street Meetings, or through the rapid growth within the FGBMFI over the last five years.

As one who has been so dependent upon the word of God since those days in Rangoon, I, like many others, am more than thankful for the important work being accomplished by such organisations as the Christian Literature Crusade, Gideons International, the Bible Society, Scripture Union and Pocket Testament League – to mention but a few that have been a personal encouragement to me through the thirty eight years since I first met my wife to be, in the far-off country of Burma.

15: Jesus is Alive Today

In the thirty eight years since first reading the New Testament the evidence from many personal testimonies and answers to prayer have confirmed that, without a doubt, this is a Living Word. Each day has proved to me more and more the importance of our utter dependence upon reading and believing the word, knowing that what God says is true, what He says He means and what He wants us to do is simply to take Him at His word and believe.

Some years ago, when I was visiting one of my clients at an Oxfordshire industrial estate, I had just slipped out from behind the steering wheel of my car when a shout drew my attention towards one of the company representatives. I think his name was Brian. Since he was an outside representative and rarely around the head office I knew him only casually. He appeared to be in a hurry to share something with me and blurted out excitedly 'I have the same Boss as you now!' At first I didn't know what he meant until he began to unfold a most intriguing series of events. We walked into the company offices and Brian directed me into the works manager's office where we were both offered seats. The works manager seemed very relaxed and almost amused as he awaited my reaction to that which Brian was about to relate. He had been directed to attend a large trade conference in Athens a few weeks back. His days during the conference were spent fully occupied with high pressure sales presentations and time and motion study methods, allowing little time for personal relaxation. However, Brian decided to slip out during one of the mid-day breaks and find quiet in a nearby park. Whilst relaxing, someone approached him and began to talk, quoting from the Bible, and, before leaving had introduced Brian to the Saviour his works manager had known for years and sought to share with him. The three of us agreed that the Lord's ways are past understanding.

Brian never saw the stranger again. I was very interested in Brian's progress especially as his interest and enthusiasm were phenomenal. He had a great desire to share his testimony with the sales force in his company; a few months later he was nominated Officer for the local Chapter of the FGBMFI in his area. To this day he never misses an opportunity when he finds representatives are booked in for a trade show the following day.

Recently, when invited to address a FGBMFI breakfast in Glasgow, I became interested in a vibrant young sales executive giving his testimony. It appeared he had only been a Christian for a few months but I heard he was engaged in the same commercial work as Brian. After the gathering, I was able to learn a little more from the sales executive. Not only was he Scottish agent for the same company but he owed his new found faith to a late night session in a hotel where he met with Brian.

Being asked to handle the editorship for the *Voice and Vision* magazine within the UK allows me ample opportunity to follow through the interesting stories coming to light each month.

Opportunities for testimony can be provided in many ways, maybe a chance to speak to one person or several dozen, or even a thousand; they are all very important and vital in every way. I recollect in my earlier days as a

Christian on holiday in Leven, Fife, I was anxious to support any evangelistic work and assembled with friends from the local Baptist church at a Sunday afternoon open air meeting. As we were singing choruses I was called upon to give a testimony. This sort of sudden request has its pros and cons depending whichever way you look at it, especially if one is of a nervous disposition. Hurriedly, I scribbled a few points on a scrap of paper. Up to this time I had rarely given testimony to a crowd, much less in the open air. The minutes ticked by and then the Minister turned to me to say a few words. I slotted my notes in my copy of Golden Bells hymn book as I rose to speak. It so happened that at this precise moment a sudden gust of wind whistled around me, and my notes were gone, down the sandy beach never to be seen again.

In situations like these one either freezes or calls on the Lord in great haste and perhaps with a slight measure of panic! How thankful I was that, as on those previous occasions in Thailand, He always answers. He brought to remembrance, in perfect sequence, the best items to help and encourage someone listening. Length of testimony is often a nightmare to many chairing a meeting, or even when a visitor is asked to say a few words during a FGBMFI dinner – it can be one is in for a well prepared sermon!

On another occasion I had been invited to give a brief testimony at one of the Late Night Specials, a popular event during the annual Christian Holiday Camp at Filey. A few days prior to the event I was asked to limit my story to fifteen minutes which I thought would be no problem. The evening duly arrived and the chairman, hastily planning a few last minute items, asked if I might curtail my few words to ten minutes. Again, I saw no problem. As the rally progressed, with at least a thousand people in the large auditorium, a formidable choir were engaged in one of the newest songs from the Scriptures. The chairman whispered to me what I hoped would be his final request, could I possibly make it in under five minutes! He confirmed this remark by informing me of the large, somewhat overbooked programme! Trying to condense three and a half years into fifteen minutes takes careful planning but squashing it into five minutes required a miracle! I had never been given so short a time to speak but, I was to learn that, under the anointing of the Holy Spirit, it is possible to say enough in so short a period. My instant prayer at that moment was once again answered.

There are times when it is important to set aside a period for intercessory prayer but in some cases an emergency arises when there is no time for long prayers. Such a situation arose when my wife and I were returning from a brief holiday in Switzerland with our pastor and his wife. We were driving through Germany, having left Darmstadt, near Frankfurt. A violent thunderstorm suddenly engulfed us in torrential rain while we were travelling at a speed relative to the other traffic. But as we approached a curve in the road, George, a very able driver, lost control of the car and we veered across and hit the central reservation, then as we bounced back off the grass verge we saw we were unavoidably skidding at right angles into the path of a lorry. We were closing rapidly and, as the lorry was about to smash into the side of the car, another car tried to avoid hitting us on the far side. The pastor's wife cried, just one word, 'JESUS'! At that precise moment Jesus answered, for suddenly the car came under control again and we found we had been wonderfully repositioned within the central line. The lorry was in the next lane, much to the surprise of the German driver. The other car was never seen again and the storm subsided as quickly as it started. With great thankfulness we dropped our speed and found a lay-by, where we praised the Lord for our amazing and immediate deliverance. What was even more remarkable was that we found, to our amazement, that not one of us had any fear or apprehension whatever, before, during or after the incident. I am almost certain that had our sister not called upon the name of Jesus, at that precise time, we would not have survived.

Prayer for healing has not always been a popular subject, and I, like others, had my own views. It is strange how the Lord arranges one's itinerary. I was invited, along with many other laymen, to support the Rev. Trevor Dearing in visiting various parts of the country. It was a privilege and a further step in my training, to witness a ministry of salvation, coupled with healing and deliverance. Often when you are pondering certain aspects of the Lord's work, He provides the answer, either from or through His word but, in some cases, during direct conversation.

It was late one evening during a salvation and healing rally at a crowded hall on the Essex coast. Having observed many needy people coming forward for individual prayer, I was giving a good deal of thought as to how many of those we had prayed for had in fact been healed or even helped in some way. A few minutes later a lady rushed from the back of the hall and excitedly started to tell me how wonderful everything was! I naturally assumed she was enjoying the final choruses prior to the benediction, but no, she, looking radiant, was telling me how great the Lord was to her. I vaguely recalled an hour earlier having ministered to her in the healing line, when she had requested prayer for her back and as I was about to pray she quickly asked me, as an afterthought, to pray also for her eye. Now she had come to tell me how, from the age of five years, one of her eyes had been completely useless and that all she experienced was a difference in shades of light or dark; her other eye was perfect. She was a lady in her late thirties and, with joy, revealed how, a few minutes earlier, the grey shades had suddenly gone leaving a clear vision of the church hall. From several of these episodes in my life I have no doubt that as the Scriptures declare, 'The Word of God is quick and powerful, and sharper than any two-edged sword.'

When counselling or ministering, it is vital to show the particular portion of scripture appropriate to each enquirer. Only the word of the Lord, empowered by the Holy Spirit, brings about the transformation needed, especially when an enquirer believes the word they have been shown.

Let me share a lovely, yet simple, episode in a family, all of whom were young Christians, and of what the Lord was able to do for them when they simply believed God. Doris, mother of two, lived close to us, and was in a desperate situation the day she shared the tragic news of her husbands' redundancy. This was before the days of redundancy pay-outs. With a young growing family, she was very anxious. But she was one of the many Christian ladies who believed and proved the power of the Lord through His word. I met her in the street near her home and confirmed what she had always believed, that the Lord would never fail her or the family. Opening my Bible I slowly and simply told her the words that were in front of me. I prefixed it, by mentioning casually that there is a telephone number you can always call, will always get a reply, it will never be engaged, or unobtainable, the line is always open and it would not cost her a penny.

Continuing, I emphasised the only condition was to accept and believe what I was giving her from the word of

God. The 'telephone number' being none other than Jeremiah 33.3, 'Call unto Me, and I will answer thee, and shew thee great and mighty things which thou knowest not'. Doris was just calling unto the Lord and knew so confidently from the Scriptures that He would answer! The word in this case was quick and sharp. Doris called me within two days with great excitement, sharing how Sam had already been given employment, so soon after his redundancy and, what was more, he had a far better job than his previous one. Doris soon began to cherish that verse, knowing that not only did the Lord answer her call but He gave her more than she had asked for. This shows the amazing way the Holy Spirit anoints the word followed by action in a particular situation.

At the close of an evening service in a Kent, Assemblies of God church, a young man in his twenties was concerned with a personal problem of some kind and hesitant to speak with me. When he did, he found he could not get round to his problem.

The Lord prompted me, during his nervousness, to hastily open my Bible and show him a verse. I invited him to read the words slowly. He did so, and then I asked him to repeat the words, a bit louder, which he did, 'Trust in the Lord with all thine heart and lean not unto thine own understanding. In all thy ways acknowledge Him and he shall direct thy paths'. As he read, I hardly had anything to say and was confirming to him that if only he would trust the Lord completely with his problem and quit leaning on his own understanding, his paths would be directed. With an exclamation his face changed from one of deep concern to one of relief and joy.

He straightened himself up to full height and making a comment, 'Praise the Lord, that's it' . . . he withdrew after a quick wave and disappeared in the crowds making their way from the church. I never did know what his problem was.

How marvellous it is when we can look into God's word with such assurance for the complete and everlasting answer. The Lord has been so wonderful in confirming to me all through my Christian life, how important His word is. Repeatedly I have seen the amazing way peoples' spiritual eyes have been opened, as they drank in the word of God. It seemed to happen at every meeting we attended and brought such joy to me, knowing that had it not been for the word of God, I would never have met with either my Nursing Sister, or my Lord!

The word of God is a strong weapon when ministering to people with depressions, as I soon found out. During one meeting I experienced a remarkable change in a lady who had been brought by her friends and her husband to discuss her problem. It was towards the end of an evening dinner function of the FGBMFI at a hotel in Essex. Her countenance was one of expressionless sadness. Little comfort was coming to her from any of the evening's praise and worship. I was discreetly informed she had been prayed for on a number of previous occasions, with little response.

Whilst several of the Officers of the Chapter gathered round her to encourage her, her blank expression gave little incentive to us, as we considered her condition before we ministered to her. I was prompted to open my Bible at the book of Isaiah, 41:10 and, in addition, to my audible reading of the verse, I invited her to read the words for herself. Slowly, she read the verse, then I asked her to read it once again. She read this in a faint voice and finally, after she read the words a third time, we pointed out to her, the simplicity of the words from the Lord to her, only asking her to believe what she was reading. The words of that verse are so encouraging and I found myself entering into them as I ministered to her.

'Fear not Sister, for the Lord is saying to you now, "I AM with you, actually with you. Don't be dismayed," He is saying 'I AM thy God and I will strengthen you and I will help you, and I will uphold you with My right hand of righteousness." As we continued to encourage her, several of us were standing together in prayer and under the anointing of the Holy Spirit took the authority contained in the Bible, to pray for her deliverance from the depression in the all-powerful name of Jesus. Within a few moments she appeared more relaxed and took a seat for a moment prior to leaving the hotel. Within fifteen minutes, as we were about to leave the dining room, it was a delight to see a happy husband leaving with his wife, who was so remarkably different from the way she had arrived hours earlier. There was a noticeable transformation upon her countenance; of peace and contentment within her expression. The dark and dull shadows had receded, transformed by the living word – providing a peace which is promised by Jesus when we come to Him – of 'perfect love, casting out all fear'.